Five Seasons of Wall Quilts

by Teresa M. Reilly

EZ INTERNATIONAL
95 Mayhill Street
Saddle Brook, NJ 07662

Dedication

This book is dedicated to my husband Lawrence and my
children Mark, Karen, Christopher, Jacqueline, and Peter for
their encouragement and help.

Acknowledgements

Special thanks to Cathy Slivinski of EZ International.

Cover design by Bud Geisenheimer, Our Way Studios, Fort Lee, New Jersey.

Photography by Brad Stanton, Danbury, Connecticut.

Graphic design and layout by Shimp Personalized Publication Services, Inc., Las Vegas, Nevada.

Published in the United States of America by EZ International, Saddle Brook, New Jersey.

Printed in Hong Kong.
98 97 96 95 94 93 10 9 8 7 6 5 4 3 2 1

ISBN: 1-881588-10-6

Table of Contents

Introduction

We always slept under quilts when we visited my grandmother. In fact, there was a quilt on every bed. When autumn came Grandma aired the quilts and put a different quilt on each bed for winter. Now we sleep under quilts on the beds in my home. Some have been made by me and some were made by my grandmother.

There are so many patterns I want to make, but I never seem to have enough time to do them all. Now I make wall quilts! They decorate the walls throughout my home. As the seasons change, I change my wall quilts.

To quiltmakers, every quilt is special because we choose our favorite colors and fabrics. I encourage you to use the patterns in this book to make your own special quilts. And always remember to sign your quilt!

The terms and techniques are defined here as I have used them in my patterns to make my quilts. They are not intended to be a complete guide to quilt making. Read through complete pattern before cutting fabric.

Fabrics should be 100% cotton except where a specialty fabric such as velvet is used. Wash all fabrics to preshrink and remove excess dye. Dark colors may "run" or "bleed". Rinse these until water is clear. Dry and iron all fabrics.

The amount of fabric required is listed with each quilt. This yardage is based on efficient use of fabric when cutting, i. e.: squares are cut in a row with cutting lines next to each other. If you are concerned about not having enough fabric buy ¼ yard more than the listed yardage. Fabric for back of quilt should be as light as the light background areas of quilt top. Avoid dark fabrics that could "shadow" through the batting.

Terms, Techniques, and Tools

Grain Line or Straight of Grain. Lengthwise: runs parallel to selvage edge with very little stretch. Crosswise: runs across width of fabric with a small amount of stretch. Bias: runs diagonally across fabric and is very stretchy. Arrows on templates are always placed on straight of fabric either lengthwise or crosswise. Always follow this arrow unless the pattern in the fabric takes priority. All fabric edges that are on the outside of square or quilt top must be cut on the "straight".

Thread. 100% cotton or cotton covered polyester thread for hand or machine piecing. Color should match fabrics. Quilting thread should be used for hand quilting. This can be 100% cotton or cotton covered polyester but is heavier than all purpose thread. Thread for appliqué always matches the color of the appliqué piece. Basting should be done with light colored thread. A single strand of thread is used for piecing, appliquéing, basting and quilting.

Needles. Use #7 or #8 betweens for hand piecing. Use #9 or #10 betweens for quilting. Use #11 or #12 sharps for appliqué. Use long thin needles such as #7 darners for basting.

Batting. Use good quality thin 100% polyester bonded batting. Measure your finished quilt top and use batting piece 2" to 4" larger all around.

Template. A quilters pattern piece. The templates given have a solid line and a dotted line. The distance between these lines is the ¼" seam allowance. For machine piecing make template from solid line. Cut fabric piece this shape and sew pieces together with accurate ¼" seams. For hand piecing make template from dotted line. Mark this sewing line on fabric and add ¼" seam allowance when cutting out pieces. Sew pieces together matching sewing lines. Use template plastic to make templates. You may use a rotary cutter and mat and Easy Angle™, Easy Angle II™ and Companion Angle™ to cut shapes

listed in the quilt patterns. Directions for using these tools are found on pages 9-10.

Marking tools. Before you mark any lines on fabric, test to make sure these lines can be removed or will rub off as you piece or quilt. Always mark just dark enough to be seen. Lines should be thin and not smudge.
  0.5 mm mechanical pencil
  Silver very thin artist pencil
  EZ Clean Erase quilting pencils
  EZ Tailors Chalk pencil – various colors

Piecing. You may choose to piece by hand or sewing machine. I do both. *Remember that accuracy is the goal.* All the pieces of your quilt must fit together perfectly. They will if you have made and followed accurate templates and sewn with ¼" seam allowances. I finger press as I piece. When top is complete I "press" up and down with an iron on the right side first. Press seams to one side toward the dark fabric. Where several seams intersect press to distribute the thickness evenly.

Appliqué instructions. Templates are made full size. Place on right side of fabric and draw around shape. Cut out with scant ¼" seam allowance. Follow any directional arrows when cutting. Draw or trace complete appliqué design onto background fabric. Pin appliqué piece to background fabric matching lines on appliqué to lines on background.

Needleturn Method: With the tip of your needle, turn under the seam allowance on the line drawn on the appliqué piece. Appliqué with blind stitch or tack stitch as follows. Use #10 sharps with 18" long thread the same color as appliqué piece. Make a small knot. Hide the knot in seam allowance on back of appliqué piece. Bring needle out through folded edge. Insert needle in background fabric directly behind this stitch. Move needle ⅛" away coming up to just catch the edge of the appliqué piece. Continue to make these small stitches that hook right over the edge of the appliqué piece. See graphic on next page.

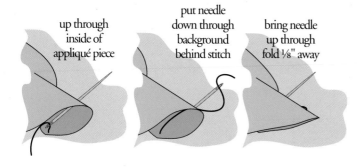

up through inside of appliqué piece

put needle down through background behind stitch

bring needle up through fold ⅛" away

Inside points: Cut to seam line. Make additional small stitches at the inside point.

Clip concave curves only as necessary for appliqué to lie flat.

Points: stitch along the edge to the point. Make several extra stitches at the point to hold it. Use needle to tuck seam allowance under. Pinch with thumb to flatten. Appliqué this edge.

Do not turn under edges that will lie under another appliqué piece. Follow order in pattern to appliqué the pieces.

When appliqué is complete, cut away the background fabric behind the whole appliqué design leaving a ¼" seam allowance. This allows the batting to fill the area and leaves only one layer of fabric to quilt through.

Check to make sure that no dark fabrics are shadowing through lighter fabrics. Trim back where necessary. End thread by taking two small stitches in seam allowance. Make sure dark threads do not shadow through background.

Circles: Paper piecing. Make circles from card weight paper. Pin paper to wrong side of fabric circle. Turn fabric over the edge and baste to paper circle. Paper shape is removed when background is cut away from finished appliqué.

Stems: Cut bias strips the desired finished width plus ⅜". Pin lengthwise center of bias strip over stem drawn on background. With needle turn under and appliqué inside curve first. Remove pins and appliqué outside curve. Do not cut out behind narrow stems.

Mitering corners. Border strips are cut the length of the quilt top plus the width of the border plus 2". If you are using several borders sew strips together first to make one border piece. Lay quilt top face up on flat surface. Center border strip to center point on quilt side. Pin border strip to quilt. Sew on border beginning and ending ¼" from each end of the quilt. Repeat with other border strips. Ends are free and extend beyond each end of quilt. With right sides together, fold adjacent border strips together matching outside edges and lining up border seams. The quilt top will be folded on the diagonal. Extend this diagonal line to mark sewing line on the border. Sew. Then open to make sure the corner lies flat. Trim seam to ¼".

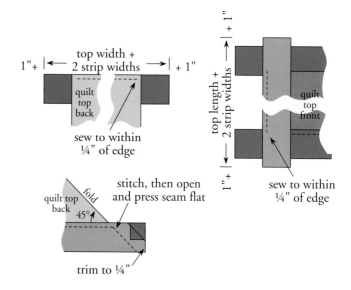

1"+ |← top width + 2 strip widths →| + 1"

quilt top back

sew to within ¼" of edge

top length + 2 strip widths

1"+

quilt top front

sew to within ¼" of edge

quilt top back

fold

45°

stitch, then open and press seam flat

trim to ¼"

Making a stencil. Trace design onto template plastic. Mark "bridges" or uncut spaces along each line so stencil will not fall apart. Use double blade cutting knife to cut out channel over lines. After marking lines on quilt fill in bridges so there is a continuous quilting line.

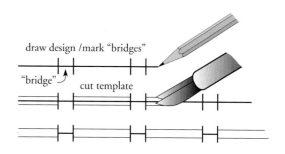

draw design /mark "bridges"

"bridge"

cut template

Stitch Thru™ is a paper template that is preprinted with quilting designs.

Sample Stitch-Thru™ Designs

Basting the quilt. Spread the backing fabric wrong side up on flat surface. Tape corners and several places along the edges to hold taut. Spread batting over the backing. Pat to smooth. Center the quilt top right side up on top of batting. Smooth. Pin layers together with straight pins 6" apart. Use long needles and white thread or basting thread to baste the three layers together. Start in the center and stitch to the edges. Secure the thread with two stitches when you start and end. Layers must be held together securely. Rows of stitches form 4" grid over the entire quilt. Baste around the outside edge of the whole quilt. Remove pins and begin to quilt!

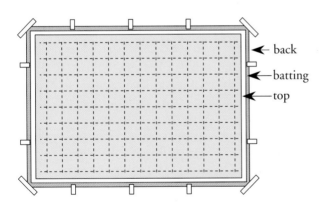

Quilting. The quilting stitch is a small evenly spaced running stitch which holds the quilt top, batting and back together. Use #9 or #10 betweens needle and 18" length of quilting thread. Make a small knot in the thread. Always work on the top of the quilt. Insert needle through the quilt top into the batting layer. Staying in the batting layer, bring the needle

forward and out through the quilt top on the quilting line where you will start quilting. Pull gently to pop the knot into the batting. Quilt, following the marked lines.

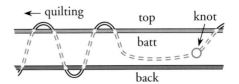

To end quilting, make a small knot in the thread 1" above the quilt surface. Insert needle through the quilt top into the batting layer going back toward quilting stitches just completed. Draw the thread back approximately 2", very close to the first row of stitching. Bring needle out on top. Pop in the knot and cut thread close to the quilt top.

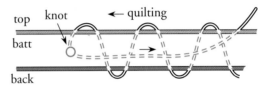

Always begin to quilt in the center of the quilt and move out in even larger circles until the quilt is completely quilted. "Quilt in the ditch" means to quilt close to the seam on the side opposite the folded seam allowance. I recommend using a 14" quilting hoop.

Finishing and binding. When all quilting is complete, lay quilt on a flat surface. Square and trim all edges even. Binding strips have been cut and sewn as directed in each quilt pattern. Fold the strips in half lengthwise with wrong sides together. Press. With quilt on flat surface, place raw edges of binding over raw edge of the quilt. Begin in the center of one side of the quilt. Leave beginning 4" of binding free. Pin binding to quilt. Stop ¼" from corner. Fold binding diagonally up and then straight down. Continue pinning binding to quilt making this fold at each corner. When ends of binding meet, cut edges on the diagonal and sew together. Refer to the graphic on the following page.

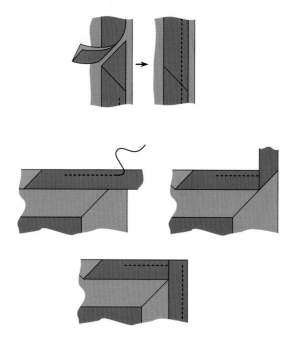

Stitch pinned binding to quilt on sewing machine with ¼" seam. Stop stitching ¼" from corner and back stitch. Lift needle and begin sewing ¼" from the corner on the next side of the quilt. Continue sewing binding to all sides of the quilt. Turn binding to back and hand sew folded edges of binding to just cover the stitching line. Fold corners to form miter in the binding.

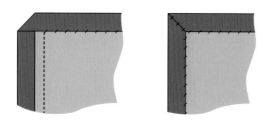

Sometimes you do not want the binding to show on the front of the quilt. Sew binding to quilt top as above. Then turn binding to back along the seam line and stitch to back of quilt. Fold corners to form a miter. *Snow Crystals* and *Arabic Lattice* have the binding turned completely to the back.

Sleeve for hanging quilt. Make a sleeve for hanging the quilt from the same fabric as the back of the quilt. Make two pieces. Leave a space in the center so that a dowel or rod may be hung from one hanger. Cut two strips 6½" wide by half the width of the quilt. Turn under and stitch 1" hems on short ends of these pieces. Fold right sides together and sew long sides together. Turn right side out. Sew these sleeves to back of the quilt as shown. Stitch by hand along both long sides. Dowel or rod goes inside sleeve and does not touch the quilt.

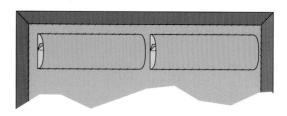

Sign and date your quilt. Use a permanent pen to write your name, date, city, state and country on the back of your quilt. An embroidered or cross stitch label or typed muslin label can be sewn to the quilt back. Your grandchildren and future generations will want to know the story of this special quilt.

Tool Tutorial – Easy Angle™ and Easy Angle II™

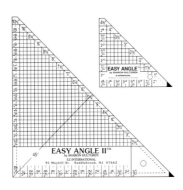

Easy Angle™ and Easy Angle II™ provide a quick method to cut right triangles for half square triangles or triangle squares. Just add seam allowance to your finished size and cut strips this width. Place two cut strips of fabric right sides together, then cut with the Easy Angle™ or Easy Angle II™. The lines on the tool are provided at ¼" increments, and are used for aligning fabric strips for cutting. The heavier lines are provided at ½" increments. Easy Angle™ yields unfinished triangles of 1" to 4½". Easy Angle II™ yields unfinished triangles of 2½" to 10½". The discussion below is for Easy Angle™, but it equally applies to Easy Angle II™.

Use of the tool requires that you select a finished square size. Once you do this, add ½" to get the corresponding unfinished triangle size. Cut strips the

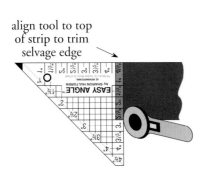

align tool to top of strip to trim selvage edge

unfinished width of the triangle size. Lay the strips right sides together. Trim selvages from strips before cutting the triangles.

For each strip or pair of strips, align the bottom of the tool over the top of the strip(s) as shown, and trim the selvage edge. Align the bottom of the

tool on the bottom edge of the strip. Slide the tool to the right until the end of the strip aligns with the strip width number along the diagonal edge. The entire number must be on the fabric. Cut along the diagonal edge of the tool.

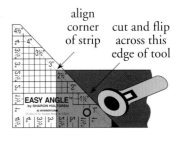

align corner of strip

cut and flip across this edge of tool

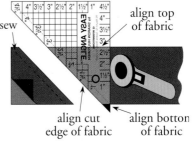

sew

align top of fabric

align cut edge of fabric

align bottom of fabric

Flip the tool over the long edge and align the tool so that the cut edge of the fabric aligns with the strip width number and the bottom edge of the fabric aligns with the top of the black triangle on the tool. Cut along the perpendicular edge of the tool.

Repeat these last two steps until you have cut all of your triangles. You will have pairs of triangles which you may chain sew to make the triangle-squares. Note that the triangles are already right sides together. Simply sew, open up and press seam to one side.

To make single fabric squares up to 4½" using Easy Angle™ (or up to 10½" using Easy Angle II™), cut a strip equal to the unfinished square size. Align the tool with the top edge of the strip and slide it along the strip until the left side of the strip aligns with the vertical line on the tool representing the unfinished square size. The entire number must be on the fabric. Cut along the vertical side of the tool.

align end of strip with unfinished square size

align top of strip with edge of tool

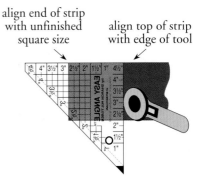

Use Companion Angle™ to cut triangles with the long edge on the outside of a block, border, or quilt. Cut the triangles with the long edge on the straight of the grain to prevent distortion.

Dashed lines represent sewing lines and show the *finished* triangle size, based on a ¼" seam allowance; center numbers represent the width of the strip to cut; solid lines underneath are used for alignment (for example, cut a 2½" strip for *finished* 4" triangles.)

Determine the required size of the long edge of your finished triangle.

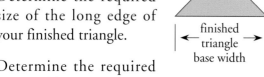

Determine the required strip width to cut to get the desired triangle size. This will be the distance from the top of the tool to the solid line immediately below the dashed line corresponding to the triangle finished base width.

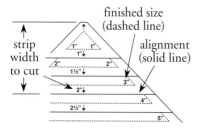

Cut strips as required. Lay the tool on top of the strip so you can read the tool name. Then align the top of the tool with the top of the strip, the appropriate solid line with the bottom of the strip. Cut on both sides to get one triangle.

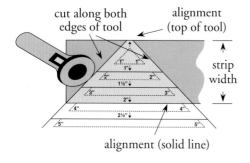

Turn the tool upside down and align the side of the tool with the end of the strip, the top of the tool with the bottom of the strip, and the top of the strip with the appropriate solid line. Cut on the right side of the tool to get the next triangle. Next, turn the tool right side up again, align and cut on the right side. Continue with these steps until you have the necessary triangles.

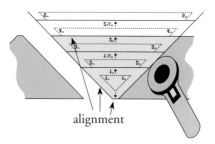

To get trapezoids, first determine the finished base or top length and the finished height. Add ½" to the finished height. Cut strips this width.

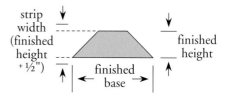

Find the dashed line on the tool labeled with the finished base or top length, and the associated solid line beneath the dashed line. Align this solid line on the bottom or top of the strip. Cut the first trapezoid by cutting on both sides. Turn the tool upside down. Line up the end of the strip with the left side of the tool and the top of the strip with the appropriate solid line. Cut along the right side of the tool. Turn the tool right side up and continue.

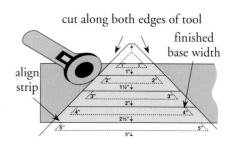

Amish Baby Quilt

42"x 50"
Pieced and quilted by Teresa Reilly.

I fell in love with this antique Amish baby quilt at an antique show. The simple triangle shapes of randomly placed pastels just sparkled. This anonymous Amish mother filled the wide border with many stitches in a traditional quilting design. Make this quilt for a special baby or display it to brighten long winter days.

Pattern block size: 3" square

REQUIREMENTS

Fabric:
Pastel mini prints and solids to equal 2 yds.
¼ yd. slate blue solid
½ yd. medium blue solid
1 yd. dark blue solid
1½ yds. backing
batting 44" x 54"

Template:
Template 4a, triangle – base 3", height 1½" (or use Companion Angle™)

Cutting:
280 template 4a triangles from assorted pastels. If you use Companion Angle™, cut the appropriate number of triangles from 2" wide fabric strips. Align the top of the tool with the top of the strip. Refer to page 10.

Borders: Cut crossgrain
Slate blue – cut 2 strips 1¾" x 30½"
Slate blue – cut 2 strips 1¾" x 24"
Dark blue – cut 2 strips 8½" x 33"
Dark blue – cut 2 stirps 8½" x 40½"
Med. blue – cut 2 strips 1¾" x 40½"
Med. blue – cut 3 strips 1¾" wide crossgrain and piece to equal 2 strips 1¾" x 52"

Binding:
Med. blue – cut 2 strips 1¾" x 40½"
Med. blue – cut 3 strips 1¾" wide crossgrain and piece to equal 2 strips 1¾" x 52"

PIECING DIRECTIONS

This is a randomly pieced quilt. There is no repeat in the arrangement of the triangles. Follow the diagram below to sew four triangles to make 70 squares.

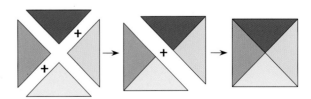

Arrange these squares in ten rows with seven squares in each row. Arrange squares to distribute color intensity throughout the quilt but not in a repeated design. Sew squares together in rows. Sew rows together to complete center panel. Patchwork is 21½" x 30½" at this point.

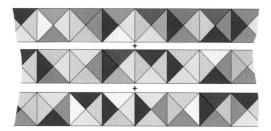

First Border: Sew the 1¾" x 30½" slate blue strips to the long sides. Then sew the 1¾" x 24" slate blue strips to the top and bottom.

Second Border: Sew the 8½" x 33" dark blue strips to the long sides. Then sew the 8½" x 40½" dark blue strips to the top and bottom.

Third Border: Sew the 1¾" x 40½" medium blue solid strips to the top and bottom. Then sew the 1¾" x 52" medium blue strips to the long sides.

QUILTING DESIGN – SQUARES

Follow the diagram below to mark quilting lines ½" in from the edge of the triangles. This quilting line forms a square set on point over the seams that join the 3" pieced squares. Extend the quilted squares into the slate blue borders.

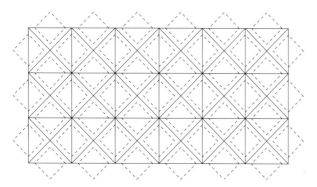

QUILTING DESIGNS – WIDE BORDERS

Make a stencil for the Amish fan quilting design or use a light box to trace the design onto fabric. Follow the diagram to mark the Amish fan design

in wide dark blue borders. Place bottom line of design on the seam line.

Place point A at right corner of each side. Mark all lines at 1, 2, 3, and 4. Place point B at 1¼" in from the left corner of each side. Mark all lines at 5, 6, 7, and 8. Mark one Amish fan in the center of the top and bottom borders (9 and 10). Mark two Amish fans on each side border (11, 12, 13, and 14). Place point A of 11 and 12 at the center of the side border and mark all lines. Add 13 and 14 last. Adjust to fit by increasing the distance between points A and B as necessary.

Corners: Continue all lines around the corners to meet line A.

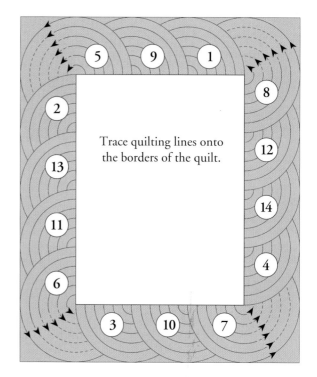

Trace quilting lines onto the borders of the quilt.

FINISHING

Layer the back, batting and quilt top. Baste following the directions on page 7. Then quilt on all marked lines.

When all the quilting is complete, square and trim all edges even. Sew the medium blue 1¾" x 40½" strips to the top and bottom. Sew the 1¾" x 52" medium blue strips to the sides. Turn this binding to the back along the seam. Turn raw edge under ¼" and stitch to the back of the quilt.

Sign and date your quilt.

Pattern block size: 4" flying geese

Sun in the Winter Woods Quilt
31" x 31"
Pieced and quilted by Teresa Reilly.

Begin with a triangle. Add corner right triangles and you have made the traditional flying geese pattern. Put rows of these "geese" together and you have created pine trees. It just follows that pine trees in winter are snow covered. Add a bright winter sun shining through this woods.

When you select your "tree" fabrics imagine dark pine trees covered with snow. Some of them now appear to be lighter shades of green. "Snow" fabrics can also range from bright white to shades of gray.

This is another wonderful scrap quilt. I used twenty-six different fabrics in this quilt. Use your collection of fabrics following the piecing chart and color photograph for placing dark, medium and light trees in your woods.

REQUIREMENTS

Fabric:

½ yd. dark green print (border & binding)
¼ yd. yellow (narrow border and sun)
¼ yd. white or white-on-white
¼ yd. light gray print
⅛ yd. dark gray print
⅛ yd. medium gray print
⅛ yd. white with gray print
⅛ yd. white with small flower print
⅛ yd. white with blue print
⅛ yd. blue gray print
⅛ yd. each of **six** dark green prints
⅛ yd. each of **five** medium green prints
⅛ yd. each of **three** light green prints
⅛ yd. each of **two** dark green solids
⅛ yd. light green solid
⅛ yd. each of **two** teal blue prints
⅛ yd. light teal blue print
⅛ yd. solid teal

The cutting chart is on the next page!

Templates:

Template 3e, 2" right triangle (or Easy Angle™)
Template 4b, triangle – 4" base, 2" height (or Companion Angle™)

Cutting:

Letter and number keys indicate placement in the quilt. Refer to the cutting chart for fabric and template cutting details. If you use Easy Angle™ and Companion Angle™, cut the appropriate number of triangles from 2½" wide fabric strips. Refer to pages 9-10.

Borders:

Yellow – cut 2 strips ¾" x 28½"
Yellow – cut 2 strips ¾" x 29"
Dark green – cut 2 strips 1¾" x 29"
Dark green – cut 2 strips 1¾" x 31½"
Dark green – cut 2" wide strips crossgrain and piece with diagonal seams to equal 134" continuous strip for binding.

Fabric	Fabric Key	Template 4B	3E
White or White-on-white	W	20	8
Yellow(s)	Y	8	
Light Gray print	G	19	9
Dark Gray print	1	4	3
White with small flower	2	4	3
Teal Blue print #1	3	6	4
Teal Blue print #2	4	4	
Teal solid	4A		4
Dark Green print #1	5	12	
Dark Green print #2	6	2	
Dark Green print #3	7	3	
Dark Green solid #1	7A	2	2
Dark Green print #4	8	7	
Dark Green solid #2	8A	2	3
Light Green print #1	9	9	
Light Green solid	9A	4	
Medium Green print #1	10	6	
Light Green print #2	11	2	
Medium Green print #2	12	4	
Medium Green print #3	13	4	
Medium Green print #4	14	4	
Medium Green print #5	15	2	
Light Green print #3	16	10	
Medium Gray print	17	4	4
White with Gray print	18	13	1
Blue Gray print	19	2	
Dark Green print #5	20	5	
Light Teal Blue print	21	2	
Dark Green print #6	22	4	
White with Blue print	23	4	1
White star*	23A	3	

* Blue Gray print may be used instead

PIECING DIRECTIONS

Lay out the entire quilt. I do this on a table covered with white fabric. Start with the bottom row. Use layout diagram on this page and the photograph to arrange the triangles. When all 14 rows are complete walk around the table and "squint" to see how your snow covered woods looks. The two triangles forming the sun should be the strongest yellow color. Move triangle "trees" around until you are pleased with the design.

Piece the rows horizontally. Be careful not to stretch the bias edges as you sew the triangles together. Sew the 14 horizontal rows together. Your "woods" will be 28½" x 28½" when pieced.

Borders: Sew the ¾" x 28½" yellow strips to the top and bottom. Then sew the ¾" x 29" yellow strips to the sides. Sew the 1¾" x 29" dark green print strips to the top and bottom. Then sew the 1¾" x 31½" dark green print strips to the sides.

Quilting Designs: Mark quilting lines ¾" inside each triangle continuing across diagonal rows. A zig-zag design is formed. Where triangles form squares, there will be a quilted square in the center as shown below.

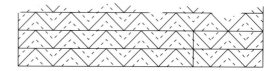

Layer, baste, quilt, square and bind. Sew sleeve to back for hanging. Don't forget to sign your quilt!

Snow Crystals Quilt

23" x 24"
Pieced and quilted by Teresa Reilly.

A visit to the "back room" of a local historical museum gave me the perfect pattern for this beautiful blue panné velvet. This is not the "spider web" pattern but "tumbling blocks". The center velvet strip is wider at one end.

Cut the velvet corners and borders to reflect light in the same or contrasting velvet nap direction.

Pattern block size: "tumbling block"
3 -3½" 60° diamonds

REQUIREMENTS

Fabric:
1 yd. blue velvet
½ yd. muslin
Assorted pieces of silk, taffeta, satin, fabric backed lamé
1 yd. black taffeta for back and binding
Batting 30" x 30"

Template:
Full size templates A, B, C, page 64

Cutting:
Note direction of nap when cutting velvet.

Velvet – cut 4 strips 3½" x 26" – borders
Black taffeta – cut 30" x 30" (back)
Black taffeta – cut 2" wide strip cross-grain and piece with diagonal seams to make 114" continuous strip for binding.

Pieces:
Velvet – cut 2 pieces from template C
Velvet – cut 2 pieces from template C *reversed*
Velvet – cut 19 pieces from template B
Silk – cut 2 pieces from template B
Muslin – cut 21 from template A

PIECING DIRECTIONS

Pin velvet piece B in the center of a muslin diamond. Follow the diagram below to randomly add pieces of silk, etc. Sew the pieces to the muslin base. Add pieces until diamond is covered. Trim the pieces even with the muslin base.

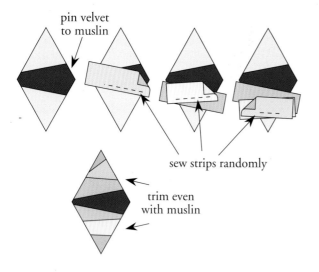

pin velvet to muslin

sew strips randomly

trim even with muslin

Make 19 diamonds with velvet centers. Make 2 diamonds with silk centers. Sew three diamonds together with the narrow end of the velvet in the center as shown. Make five of these "tumbling blocks".

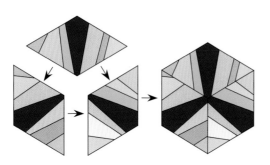

Follow the diagram to the right to piece the "tumbling blocks" together. Set-in single diamonds to complete a large "crystal". Sew corners to the pieced center.

BORDER, QUILTING, FINISHING

Borders: Sew 4 border strips to the quilt following the directions for mitered corners on page 6. Place velvet to reflect light as desired.

Quilting: No marking is required. Quilt in the ditch on both sides of the velvet center pieces. Quilt around each diamond and inside of the border. Do not quilt seam lines of the silk.

Layer the back, batting and quilt top. Baste following the directions on page 7. Quilt as described in the previous paragraph.

Finish and bind the quilt following directions on pages 7-8. Turn full width of binding to the back of the quilt. Sew sleeve on back for hanging.

Sign and date your quilt.

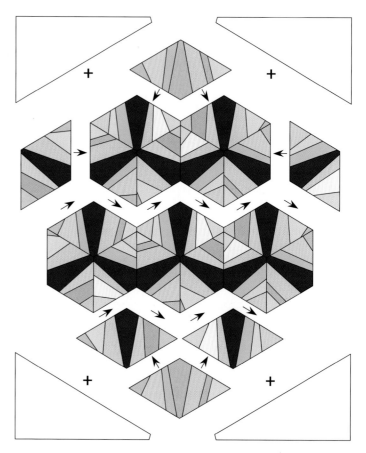

Log Cabin Pineapple Quilt

32" x 32"

Pieced and quilted by Teresa Reilly.

This pattern is called "log cabin" because each block starts with a center square "chimney" surrounded by "log" strips. Four blocks are set together for the quilt. The four purple "pineapples" meet in the center with their "green leaf crowns" extended into the corners.

There are only straight lines in the patchwork, but as you look at this quilt you see curves. Look at the pineapples. Then look at the light oval areas. Do you see a circle? This is a wonderful example of illusion and movement created from straight strips of fabric.

Pattern block size: 12" square

REQUIREMENTS

Fabric:

A – ⅛ yd. pink solid

B – ¼ yd. purple print – "pineapple"

C – ½ yd. light blue solid

D1, D2 – ⅛ yd. each of 2 medium purple prints

D3, D4 –⅛ yd. each of 2 dark purple prints

E – ⅛ yd. solid purple

F1 – ⅛ yd light green solid

F2 – ⅛ yd medium green solid

F3 – ⅛ yd medium green solid

G1 – ⅛ yd light lavender print

G2 – ⅛ yd medium lavender solid

H1-H4 – ⅛ yd each of 4 dark green prints

J – ⅛ yd solid dark green

¼ yd. slate blue solid

¾ yd. teal blue solid

1 yd. for backing

batting 35" x 35"

Template:

Template 1c, 2" square

Template 3f, 3" right triangle

Full size templates for triangle #1 and log strips #2-6. Add ¼" seam allowance to templates, page 65.

Cutting:

Cut all strips crossgrain of fabric.

Borders:

Slate blue solid – cut 2 strips 1½" x 24½"

Slate blue solid – cut 2 strips 1½" x 26½"

Teal blue solid – cut 2 strips 3½" x 26½"

Teal blue solid – cut 2 strips 3½" x 32½"

Teal blue solid – cut 2" wide strips crossgrain of fabric. Piece with diagonal seams to make 140" continuous strip for binding.

Cutting Chart

FABRIC	1c	1	2	3	3f	4	5	6
A	4				4			
B		4	4	4	8	4	4	4
C		8	8	8		8	8	
D1			8					
D2				8				
D3						8		
D4							8	
E								8
F1		8						
F2			8					
F3				8				
G1						8		
G2							8	
H1		4						
H2				4				
H3						4		
H4							4	
J					4			4

PIECING DIRECTIONS

There are four squares pieced in the same order. Lay out each square completely before sewing it together. Use the photograph and chart below for color/fabric placement.

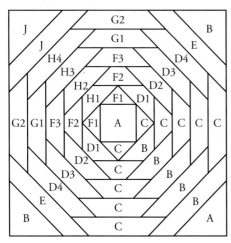

Like the traditional log cabin, first triangles then log strips are sewn around the "chimney" square. Assemble in the following steps:

1. Sew #1 triangles to each side of 1c square;
2. Sew #2 trapezoids to the corners;
3. a. Sew #3 trapezoids to the sides;
   b. Sew #3 trapezoids to the corners;
4. a. Sew #4 trapezoids to the sides;
   b. Sew #4 trapezoids to the corners;
5. a. Sew #5 trapezoids to the sides;
   b. Sew #5 trapezoids to the corners;
6. a. Sew #6 trapezoids to the sides;
   b. Sew #6 trapezoids to the corners;
7. Sew 3f triangles to the corners.

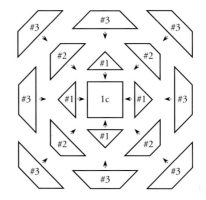

For each round #3 through #6, sew top, bottom, and side trapezoids, and then corner trapezoids.

Sew four completed blocks together matching pink corner triangles in the center. Sew 1½" x 24½" slate blue strips to the top and bottom. Sew 1½" x 26½" slate blue strips to each side. Sew 3½" x 26½" teal blue strips to the top and bottom. Sew 3½" x 32½" teal blue strips to both sides.

BORDERS, QUILTING, FINISHING

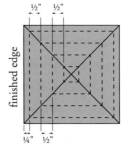

finished edge

Quilt all seam lines in the ditch including both sides of the slate blue border. Follow the diagram above to mark quilting lines in the center pink square and small pink squares.

Mark the scallop quilting design on the wide teal blue borders and corners following the directions with scallop template found on the pullout section.

Layer the back, batting and quilt top. Baste, quilt, square and bind. Sew sleeve on the back and don't forget to sign and date your quilt.

Purple Tulips Quilt
22" x 48"
Appliquéd and quilted by Teresa Reilly.

The new colors in the 1920's and 1930's were pastels. Flowers of all kinds were popular for appliqué designs. I designed my purple tulips using these soft colors. This is an easy beginning appliqué project.

Pattern block size: 12½" square

REQUIREMENTS

Fabric:
½ yd. white print
¼ yd. dark purple print
¼ yd. medium purple print
¼ yd. medium purple pin dot print
small scraps for tulip centers
¼ yd. green print for leaves and stems
¼ yd. medium purple print for border
¼ yd. yellow solid for border
½ yd. green print for border and binding
1½ yds. for back
batting 28" x 54"

Templates: Full size templates on pullout sheet
Tulip 1; Tulip 2/3
Tulip center; Tulip leaf
12½" square appliqué background

Make templates for tulip 1, tulip 2/3, tulip center, leaf. Do not add seam allowance to template.

Place template on right side of fabric. Draw around template. Cut out with scant ¼" seam allowance.

CUTTING CHART

Fabric	Borders Cut Crossgrain	Tulip Flower 1	Tulip Flower 2/3	Tulip Flower Ctr	Leaves Reg.	Leaves Reverse
Med. purple	4 - 1" x 13" 2 - 1" x 40" 4 - 1½" squares		3			
Med. purple pin dot			3			
Dark purple		3				
Purple scraps				9		
Yellow	2 - 1½" x 14" 2 - 1½" x 40"					
Green print	2 - 3¼" x 42½" 2 - 3¼" x 22"				3	3

Additional Cutting:

Green print – cut 2" wide strips crossgrain and piece with diagonal seams to make 150" continuous strip for binding.

White print – cut 3 -13½" squares – appliqué background

Green print – cut ¾" wide strips *on the bias* to make 9 strips each 6" long

APPLIQUÉ DIRECTIONS

Fold each 13½" square in half vertically and horizontally. Finger press to mark center and fold lines. Center each white print background square on top of the tulip drawing found on the pullout sheet. Trace the whole pattern. Read appliqué instructions found on pages 5-6.

Follow this order to appliqué all the pieces:

Stems: Right, left, and center. Extend the stems under the tulips, leaves, and each other by ¼".

Tulip centers: Do not turn under the bottom edge covered by the tulip.

Tulips, left leaf and then **right leaf**. Pin the pieces to the white background square matching lines drawn on the appliqué piece to lines drawn on the background fabric.

Appliqué using the needleturn method and matching color thread.

When appliqué is complete cut out the background fabric behind the appliqué. Do not cut out behind the stems.

Cut completed squares to 13" x 13".

BORDERS

Follow the diagram below and these instructions to add borders:

• Sew 1" x 13" medium purple strips to the top of each square.

• Sew squares together in long row and sew 1" x 13" medium purple strip to the bottom.

• Sew 1" x 40" medium purple strips to each side.

• Sew 1½" x 14" yellow strips to the top and bottom.

• Sew 1½" x 1½" medium purple squares to each end of the 1½" x 40" yellow strips.

• Sew these strips to the sides of the quilt.

• Sew 3¼" x 42½" green print strips to each side.

• Sew 3¼" x 22" green strips to top and bottom.

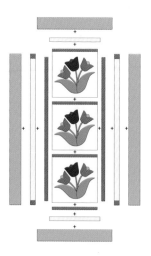

QUILTING DESIGN

Draw diagonal lines 1½" apart across the background squares. Do not draw across the appliqué. Quilt in the ditch around the tulips, stems and leaves. Quilt in the ditch on each side of all the border strips.

BORDER QUILT DESIGNS

Copy the border quilting design from the pullout sheet and go over with a black pen.

Place the design behind the green print top and corners and side borders and trace. The hashmarks indicate alignment for repeating the side tulips. Alternate tracing tulips facing inward and outward. The last tulip on each side will face inward. Adjust curved line to meet bottom corner. Adjust the corner curved line to meet side curved line.

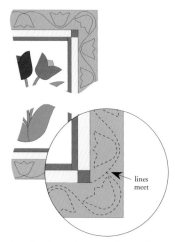
lines meet

Layer the back, batting and quilt top and baste together. Quilt, square and bind. Don't forget to sign and date your quilt.

North Carolina Lily Quilt

27" x 60"
Pieced and quilted by Teresa Reilly.

Today this pattern is usually called North Carolina Lily. Cleveland Lily was probably the name given to the red and green "lily" quilt made by members of my family in Ohio. Hand dyed fabrics inspired me to make my own "lily" quilt.

Pattern block size: 12" "lily" square set on point

REQUIREMENTS

Fabric:

1¾ yd. yellow on yellow print

1¾ yd. sage green solid

¼ yd. blue for flower pot

1¾ yd. deep pink for petals & borders

½ yd. purple for petals

2 yds. for backing

batting 31" x 64"

Note: I used hand dyed fabrics for the petals. Try some unusual fabrics in bright spring pastels.

Templates:

Template 1f, 1¾" square

Template 2a, 1¾" right triangle

Template 2b, 2½" right triangle

Template 2c, 3½" right triangle

Template 2g, 4¼" right triangle

Template 3i, 6" right triangle

Template 1m, 1¾" diamond

Template 3a, 3½" x 4¼" rectangle

Template 3c, 8½" x 1¾" rectangle

Note: You may use Easy Angle™ and Easy Angle II™ to cut the right triangles. Follow directions on page 9 for cutting triangles with these tools.

Before following the cutting chart you need to cut the following pieces:

Borders: Cut all long border strips lengthwise of fabric before cutting the other pieces!

Sage green solid – cut 2 strips 1½" x 62½"

Sage green solid – cut 2 strips 1½" x 28½"

Deep pink – cut 2 strips 1½" x 62½"

Deep pink – cut 2 strips 1½" x 28½"

Yellow – cut 2 strips 3½" x 62½"

Yellow – cut 2 strips 3½" x 28½"

Yellow – cut 2" wide strips crossgrain and piece with diagonal seams to make 184" continuous strip for binding.

Patchwork pieces:

Green – cut strips ⅝" wide *on the bias* to equal 9 strips each 6" long.

Four corners and side triangles:

Yellow – cut four 8½" right triangles *plus* ¼" seam allowance.

Yellow – cut four 12" right triangles *plus* ¼" seam allowance. *Place the diagonal edge on straight of fabric.*

CUTTING CHART

FABRIC AND TEMPLATE NUMBER

Fabric	1f	2a	2b	2c	2g	3i	1m	3a	3c
Blue		6				3			
Pink							26		
Purple							26		
Green			9						
Yellow	9	18*		3	6			3	6

*Place diagonal edge on straight of fabric.

APPLIQUÉ DIRECTIONS

Place yellow fabric rectangle over template 3a. Trace stem lines onto yellow fabric.

Follow appliqué instructions on pages 5-6.

Appliqué the bias cut green stems on to this rectangle using green matching thread. Finished stem is ¼" wide.

PIECING DIRECTIONS

It is very important to piece this block accurately. Match sewing lines exactly. Take special care not to stretch bias edges. Follow the sequence below to piece.

- Make 13 petal units from the pink and purple **1m** diamonds.

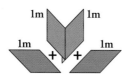

- Use these to make 9 flower units by adding the **2b** green triangles.

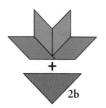

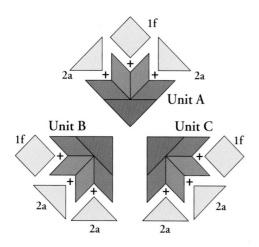

- With the flower units make three each of **Unit A, B, and C** using the yellow **2a** triangles and yellow **1f** squares.

- Sew **2g** yellow triangles to the bottom right and left sides of the completed **Unit A's** to make three of **Unit D**.

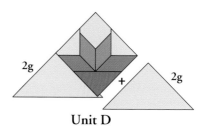

- Make 3 stem units using the **3a** rectangles. Sew **Unit B** and **C** to the sides to make the **Lily Stem Units**.

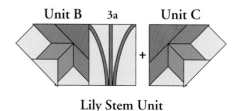

- Combine **Unit D** and **Lily Stem Units** with blue **3i** triangles.

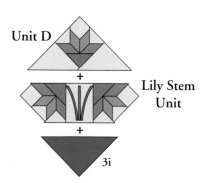

- Sew blue **2a** triangles to ends of yellow **3c** rectangles to get mirror image pieces. Sew these to the bottom right and left sides of the squares completed above. Sew yellow **2c** triangles to the bottom to complete the lily squares.

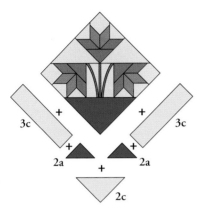

Side triangles: Center a petal unit on the diagonal side of each side triangle. Appliqué turning under the ¼" seam allowance. Use matching color thread. Do not turn under petals on seam edge side.

Diagonal Set: Sew all the quilt squares together. These lily squares are set on point. Squares, side, and corner triangles are sewn together in diagonal rows. Follow the diagram below for piecing order.

Borders: Make top and bottom border strips by sewing the 28½" long strips together green to pink to yellow. Make side border strips by sewing the 62½" long strips together green to pink to yellow. Sew the four border strips to the quilt following directions for mitered corners on page 6.

Quilting Designs: All of the lily shapes are quilted in the ditch and ¼" away from the seam lines. Do not quilt the seams where the lily square and side and corner triangles are joined.

A feathered wreath variation is used in the corners and around the appliquéd petals along the sides of the quilt. Copy the quilting designs from the pullout sheet. Go over lines with a black pen. Place this wreath design under the quilt. Trace these quilting lines in the side and corner triangles.

Quilt in the ditch on both sides of the green and pink borders. Copy the border rope quilting design from the pullout sheet. Go over these lines with a black pen. Place this design under borders and trace. Begin marking in corners and move toward the center. When you reach the center you may need to adjust the size of a rope section to fit the space available.

Layer, baste, quilt, square and bind. Sign your quilt and sew a sleeve to the back.

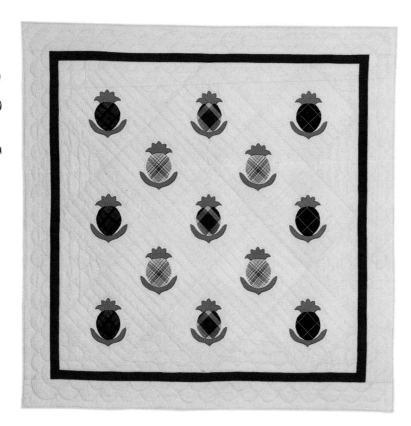

Plaid Pineapples Quilt

42" x 42"

Appliquéd and quilted by Teresa Reilly.

This easy appliqué pineapple quilt is a fun way to use small pieces of plaid fabric. If you have a good supply make each pineapple from a different plaid.

The bold colorful plaids contrast with the textured design in the quilting. Straight lines accent the diagonal placement of pineapples while quilted scallops soften the edge triangles and wide borders.

Pattern block size: 8" square with pineapple appliqué set on point.

REQUIREMENTS

Fabric:

¼ yd. each of four plaid fabrics

½ yd. solid green

¼ yd. burgundy red solid or dark solid that complements the plaids

2¾ yds. beige mini print for background, border and binding

1¼ yds. unbleached muslin or the same mini print used in the quilt top for the back

batting 45" x 45"

Templates:

A – leaf crown

B – pineapple

C – bottom leaf

8" square for appliqué background

8" right triangle (or use Easy Angle™ II)

Template 4c, triangle with base of 8" and height of 4"

Make Templates A, B, and C from full size pineapple design found on page 66. Place template on right side of the fabric. Arrow on template indicates straight of grain. Draw around the template and cut out with a scant ¼" seam allowance.

Additional Cutting:

Borders:

Beige mini print – cut 13 -9" squares

Beige mini print – cut 8 - 8½" right triangles. This includes seam allowance. *Place diagonal edge on straight of grain.* This is necessary so that all side edges of the quilt center will be on the straight of grain.

Beige mini print – cut 2 strips 3½" x 35½"

Beige mini print – cut 2 strips 3½" x 42"

Beige mini print – cut 2"wide strips cross-grain and piece with diagonal seams to make 180" continuous strip for binding.

Burgundy red – cut 2 strips 1½" x 33½"

Burgundy red – cut 2 strips 1½" x 35½"

CUTTING CHART

Fabric	A	B	C	4c
Solid green	13		13	
Plaid #1		3		
Plaid #2		4		
Plaid #3		3		
Plaid #4		3		
Beige mini				4*

*Cut as right triangle.

APPLIQUÉ DIRECTIONS

Make 13 pineapple squares. Draw a 9" x 9" square on a piece of white paper. Draw diagonal lines from corner to corner. Mark center where lines cross. Turn paper on point and place over pineapple appliqué drawing matching centers. Diagonal line will go through center of leaf crown and tip of bottom leaf. Trace complete pineapple onto paper with dark pen.

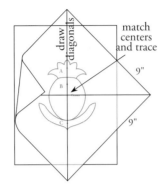

Fold each 9" background fabric square on both diagonals. Finger press to mark center and diagonal lines. Place each background fabric square on top of pineapple pattern square. Match center and diagonal lines. Trace the complete pineapple. Read appliqué instructions on pages 5-6. Pin leaf crown A to background square matching sewing lines on A with lines drawn on background square. Appliqué using needleturn method and matching green thread. Do no turn under bottom edge of A. It will be covered with top of B.

Pin pineapple B to background square matching the sewing lines on B to lines drawn on background square. Cover the seam allowance of the bottom edge of A. Appliqué all edges of pineapple B.

Pin leaf C to background square matching the sewing lines on C to lines drawn on background square. The upper edge of C fits next to pineapple B. All edges of C are appliquéd. Appliqué all 13 pineapple squares.

When appliqué is completed cut away the background fabric behind the whole design leaving ¼" seam allowance. This allows the batting to fill the area and leaves only one layer of fabric to quilt through. Cut each completed appliquéd square to 8½" x 8½".

PIECING DIRECTIONS

Diagonal Set: These pineapple squares are set on point. The squares, the side triangles and corner triangles are sewn together in diagonal rows. Refer to the diagram that follows for piecing order.

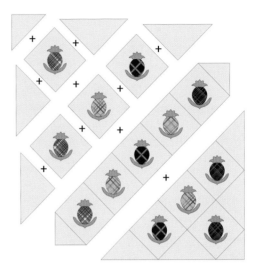

Borders: Sew a 1½" x 33½" burgundy strip to each side of the quilt. Sew a 1½" x 35½" burgundy strip to the top and bottom.

Sew a 3½" x 35½" beige background fabric strip to each side. Sew a 3½" x 42" beige background fabric strip to the top and bottom.

Quilting Design: Quilt in the ditch around all the edges of the appliquéd pineapples. Quilt ¼" outside the shape of the pineapples. Mark diagonal lines 1" apart across the background of all the pineapple squares. Do not quilt through the pineapples.

Make a quilting template for scallop quilting lines and corners following directions on pullout sheet. Mark scallop quilting lines in side triangles, corners and outside borders using quilting template. Quilt in the ditch on both sides of burgundy border.

Layer the back, batting and quilt top. Baste together. Quilt, square and bind. Sew sleeve on back of quilt for hanging. Sign and date your quilt.

Pineapple Quilt

12½" x 12½"
Appliquéd and quilted by Teresa Reilly.

From colonial times the pineapple has symbolized hospitality. Make "welcome" special with this small appliquéd pineapple wall quilt. Choose fabric with a pattern that resembles a real pineapple. Use the printed fabric design for your quilting lines.

REQUIREMENTS

Fabric:

¼ yd. green mini print

¼ yd. "pineapple" print for pineapple and border

½ yd. unbleached muslin for the background, back and binding

batting 15" x 15"

CUTTING CHART

FABRIC AND TEMPLATE

Fabric	A	B	C
Green mini	1		1
Pineapple		1	

Templates: Full size Pineapple Design

A – leaf crown

B – pineapple

C – bottom leaf

8" square for appliqué background

Make Templates A, B, and C from full size pineapple design found on page 66. Place template on right side of the fabric. Arrow on template indicates straight of grain. Draw around

the template and cut out with a scant ¼" seam allowance.

Additional cutting:

Green mini print – cut 2 strips 1" x 8½"

Green mini print – cut 2 strips 1" x 9½"

"Pineapple" print – cut 2 strips 2¼" x 9½"

"Pineapple" print – cut 2 strips 2¼" x 14"

Muslin – cut 1 -9½" square

Muslin – cut 2" wide strips crossgrain and piece with diagonal seams to equal 64" continuous strip for binding.

Muslin – cut 18" x 18" for back

APPLIQUÉ DIRECTIONS

Fold 9½" muslin background square in half vertically and horizontally. Finger press to mark center and fold lines. Place over pineapple appliqué design on page 66. Match centers and directional arrow to vertical fold line. This pineapple is centered in the square. Trace the complete pineapple.

Appliqué the complete pineapple following directions in *Plaid Pineapples*. When appliqué is completed cut away the background fabric behind the whole design leaving a ¼" seam allowance. Cut completed appliquéd square to 8½" x 8½".

Borders: Sew a 1" x 8½" strip green mini print to each side of the square and a 1" x 9½" strip green mini print to top and bottom.

Sew a 2¼" x 9½" strip of "pineapple" print to each side and a 2¼" x 14" strip of pineapple print to the top and bottom.

Quilting: Follow lines or shapes in pineapple fabric design to quilt the pineapple. Mark diagonal lines ½" apart across the background of pineapple square. Do not mark lines through pineapple. Quilt in the ditch around whole pineapple and on both sides of the green print border. Mark 1" diagonal grid in wide border or use fabric design as a guide.

Layer, baste, quilt, square and bind. Turn full width of binding to the back of the quilt. Add a sleeve for hanging. Don't forget to sign and date the quilt!

Summer Windows Quilt

42" x 38"

Appliquéd, pieced and quilted by Teresa Reilly.

If you ever vacationed by the ocean you will understand why I designed this quilt. Look through "attic windows" to see sailboats and lighthouses.

Pattern block size: 12" lighthouse square; 12" sailboat square; 4" attic window frame

REQUIREMENTS

Fabric:

¾ yd. dark red print – border

½ yd. dark blue print – window frame

½ yd. light blue and white print – window frame

½ yd. light blue print – sky

¼ yd. tan print – sand

¼ yd. blue for water. If you use moiré as I did you will need ½ yd. to cut rectangles lengthwise for design.

½ yd. white

1¼ yds. for backing

batting 45" x 45"

Templates:

Template 3e, 2" right triangle or Easy Angle™

Template 3g, 4" right triangle or Easy Angle™

Rectangles: 2" x 8"; 2" x 12"; 4" x 16"

Full size lighthouse appliqué templates, A-L made from the drawing on pullout sheet.

CUTTING CHART FOR TEMPLATE 3e AND 3g

Fabric	Template 3e	Template 3g
White		8
Light blue print	4	8
Dark blue print	4	

Cutting: Before cutting triangles from the chart it is necessary to cut strips and rectangles. All strips are cut crossgrain.

Borders: Dark red print

cut 2 strips 3¼" x 38"

cut 2 strips 3¼" x 36½"

cut 2" wide strips crossgrain and piece with diagonal seams to make 170" continuous strip for binding

Attic Window Frames:

Dark blue print – cut 3 strips 4½" wide. From these strips cut 4 rectangles 4½" x 16½" and 1 rectangle 4½" x 32½".

Light blue and white print – cut 2 strips 4½" wide. From these strips cut 4 rectangles 4½" x 16½".

Sailboat Blocks: Light blue print – sky

cut 4 rectangles 2½" x 8½"

Sailboat Blocks: Blue – water

cut 2 rectangles 2½" x 12½"

Sailboat Blocks: Dark blue print – boat

cut 2 rectangles 2½" x 8½"

Lighthouse Blocks: Light blue print – sky

cut 2 rectangles 8½" x 12½"

Lighthouse Blocks: Blue – water

cut 2 rectangles 4½" x12½"

Appliqué Cutting: Lighthouse appliqué. Copy the lighthouse templates A-L located on the pullout sheet. Do not add seam allowance to appliqué templates.

Place template on right side of fabric. Draw around template. Add ¼" seam allowance when cutting out the pieces.

White – cut 2 each A, B, C, D
Dark blue print – cut 2 each E, F, G, H, I, J
Dark red print – cut 2 from K
Tan print – cut 2 from L

PIECING DIRECTIONS – SAILBOAT BLOCKS

Follow the diagram below to piece the sailboat.

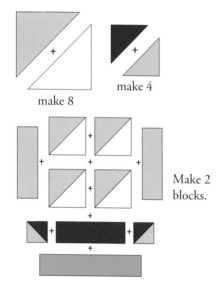

make 8   make 4

Make 2 blocks.

PIECING AND APPLIQUÉ – LIGHTHOUSE BLOCKS

Piece the lighthouse towers: Sew base of dark blue print piece E to one long side of white piece A. Match the center of the other long side of white piece A to the center of the long side of red print piece K. Sew A to K beginning and ending ¼" from ends of A.

To the other long side of red print piece K sew the longer side of white piece B. Sew the shorter side of white piece B to the top of white piece C.

Piece two houses: Sew the longer side of dark blue print F to the top side of white piece D to complete each house.

Appliqué the lighthouse block: Make 2 background squares by sewing the 12½" edge of sky fabric to the 12½" edge of water fabric. Fold each sky/water square in half horizontally and vertically. Finger press to mark center and fold lines.

Place each square on top of pattern matching center and pressed lines. Trace the complete drawing including sand line.

Place each white fabric piece C over pattern and trace window J and door I. Lightly mark the center point of 12" square and several dots along the vertical and horizontal lines to use in placing appliqué on background.

Place each white fabric piece D over pattern and trace widow H and door G.

Read appliqué instructions on pages 5-6. Appliqué dark blue print H and J windows and I and G doors using dark blue matching thread. Do not turn under the bottom edges of the doors. This edge will be covered with the sand appliqué.

Sew the house to the left side of the tower stopping ¼" from the top of the house roof. This leaves the roof seam allowance free to be turned under when appliquéd.

Place pieced lighthouse on background square matching center point, horizontal and vertical lines. Pin securely or baste to background square.

Appliqué lighthouse to background square using needleturn appliqué method. Use thread color to match appliqué piece (red, navy blue, white). Do not turn under the bottom edge. It will be covered with "sand".

Match bottom of sand piece L to bottom of square. Baste across this edge. Appliqué curved edge of sand using matching thread.

Make two lighthouse blocks. Cut away the background fabric behind all appliqué pieces including the "water" behind the "sand" and the white fabric behind the windows and doors.

ATTIC WINDOWS

The traditional attic window pattern frame is sewn to each completed block. Pin a 4½" x 16½" dark print rectangle to the left side of each 12½" block matching edges at the top with 4½" extending below the block. Sew together, ending ¼" before bottom of the block.

Pin a 4½" x 16½" light blue and white print rectangle to the bottom of each 12½" block matching the lower right edges with 4¼" extending beyond the block at the lower left corner. Sew together ending ¼" before left corner.

Fold the block diagonally so that the extended border strips can be mitered. See mitered corners, page 6. Trim mitered seam to ¼".

Sew the blocks together with a sailboat block in the upper left and lower right corners, and a lighthouse block in the remaining corners. Refer to the layout shown below for block placement and borders.

Sew the 4½" x 32½" dark blue print strip to the right side of the pieced quilt. Sew the 3¼" x 36½" dark red print strips to the top and bottom. Sew 3¼" x 38" dark red strips to each side.

QUILTING DESIGNS AND FINISHING

Sailboat blocks: Quilt wave lines in the water or quilt following the pattern in the moiré fabric. Quilt in the ditch around sails, boat and water. Quilt three lines evenly spaced diagonally across each sail. Quilt two lines along the top to the boat ¼" and ¾" from the top. Quilt in the ditch around the block.

Lighthouse blocks: Quilt in the ditch around all shapes. Quilt wave lines in the water or quilt following the pattern in the moiré fabric. Quilt three lines ½" apart following the curve of the sand. Refer to the appliqué pattern for the lighthouse quilting lines. Notice how the angled lines give a rounded look to the tower. Why not add clouds and birds in the sky?

Attic Window frames: Starting at the block edge mark a quilting line ¼", 1¼" and 2½" in both dark and light framing strips. These lines accent the depth created by the window frame as they meet at the corner.

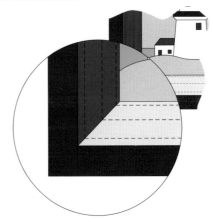

Border: Make a quilting template from the wave design found on the pullout sheet. Place the bottom of the template on the inside edge of the red border at the corner. Draw around the wave. Repeat the wave design to fill each border side. Place the wave curve in the corner and draw line to join it to the other waves. You may have to adjust the orientation and the length of the connecting lines for a smooth transition around the corner. Refer to the figure above as an example.

Layer, baste, quilt, square and bind your quilt. Sew a sleeve to the back of the quilt. Don't forget to sign and date your quilt.

Kimono T Quilt
36" x 54"
Pieced and quilted by Teresa Reilly.

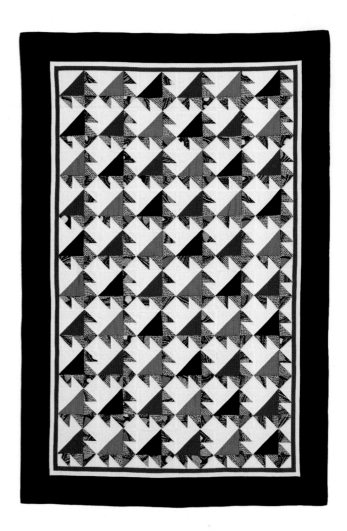

The T-square pattern has always appealed to me because of my name. My Japanese students see this graphic design as a kimono. A piece of Japanese blue and white shibori fabric was the inspiration to make my own kimono T quilt. Combine any dramatic large scale print with solid triangles to make your kimonos. The white areas also form the T shape which mirrors and interlocks with the patterned kimono T's.

Pattern block size: 4½" square

REQUIREMENTS

Fabric:
1½ yds. white
1½ yds. navy solid
½ yd. red solid
¼ yd. slate blue solid
¾ yd. navy and white print
1¾ yds. white for back
batting 42" x 60"

Templates:
Template 3f, 3" right triangle or Easy Angle™
Template 2e, 1½" right triangle or Easy Angle™

CUTTING CHART FOR TEMPLATE 3f AND 2e

Fabric	Template 3f	Template 2e
White	60	300
Navy solid	20	
Red solid	20	
Slate blue solid	20	
Navy & white print		300

Strip Cutting: Before cutting the triangles, it is necessary to cut strips. In this project not all of the strips are cut crossgrain of the fabric. Pay attention to the instructions.

Borders: White
cut 2 strips 1" x 46½" lengthwise
cut 2 strips 1" x 29½" lengthwise

Borders: Navy solid
cut 2 strips 3¾" x 47½" lengthwise
cut 2 strips 3¾" x 35½" lengthwise
cut 2" wide strips crossgrain and piece with diagonal seams to equal 200" continuous strip for binding.

Borders: Red solid
cut 2 strips 1" x 28½"
cut 4 strips 1" wide crossgrain. Piece strips end to end to make 2 long strips. From these long strips cut 2 strips 1" x 45½" long with seams in center of strips.

PIECING DIRECTIONS

Sew the small white and the small navy and white print triangles together to make 300 squares.

 Sew the large white and large red solid triangles together to make 20 squares. Sew the large white and large navy solid triangles together to make 20 squares. Sew the large white and large slate blue triangles together to make 20 squares.

Follow the diagram below to make Kimono T squares.

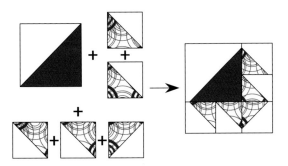

Follow the diagram below to arrange the completed Kimono T squares according to the color of the large triangles. Sew 6 squares together across each row. Repeat the first 3 rows 3 times and end with the first row. Sew the ten completed rows together. Quilt should measure 27½" x 45½".

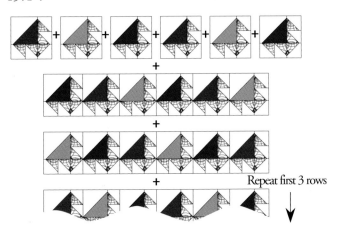

Repeat first 3 rows

BORDERS

Sew the 1" x 45½" red strips to the long sides. Then sew the 1" x 28½" red strips to the top and bottom.

Sew the 1" x 46½" white strips to the long sides. Then sew the 1" x 29½" white strips to the top and bottom.

Sew the 3¾" x 47½" navy strips to the long sides. Then sew the 3¾" x 35½" navy strips to the top and bottom.

QUILTING DESIGN

Follow the diagram to mark quilting lines ¼" away from seams to outline shapes. Do not quilt in the solid navy, red and slate blue triangles. Quilt in the ditch on both sides of the border strips.

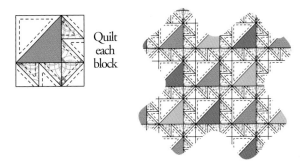

Quilt each block

Layer, baste, quilt, square and bind. Basting, quilting and binding instructions are found on pages 7-8. Finish with a sleeve on the back and don't forget to sign and date your quilt!

Ocean Waves Quilt

26½" x 66½"

Appliquéd, pieced and quilted by Teresa Reilly.

East meets West in this sharing of ocean patterns. The Oriental wave design is appliquéd in the center square of our Ocean Waves patchwork pattern. Traditional dark blue Japanese fabrics are used for piecing wave triangles. A new American textile is used for the wave appliqué.

Pattern block size: 20" square

REQUIREMENTS

Fabric:

3½ yds. white or white on white print

1¼ yd. dark blue print

½ yd. light blue print for appliqué wave

batting 32" x 72"

Templates:

Template 2b, 2½" right triangle or Easy Angle™

Template 3h, 5" right triangle or Easy Angle™

7" square appliqué background

7" right triangle or use Easy Angle II™

Wave appliqué – templates 1-12, page 67.

Before cutting the triangles, it is necessary to cut strips, squares, right triangles and rectangles.

CUTTING CHART FOR TEMPLATE 2b AND 3h

Fabric	Template 2b	Template 3h
White	144	4
Dark blue	144	

Borders and Back: White

cut 1 rectangle 34" x 72" lengthwise of fabric for back of quilt

cut 2 border strips 3½" x 60½" for sides

cut 2 border strips 3½" x 26½" for top and bottom

Pieces: White

cut 3 -8" squares for appliqué background. After appliqué is completed, each square is cut to 7½".

cut 4 -7½" right triangles. This includes ¼" seam allowance. Cut with diagonal side of triangle on straight of fabric.

Pieces: Dark blue print

cut 2" wide strips crossgrain and piece with diagonal seams to equal 210" continuous strip for binding.

PIECING DIRECTIONS

Piece white and dark blue small triangles together to make 120 squares. Follow piecing diagram to make units A through H and left and right side triangle units:

Make 120 squares

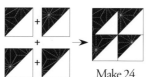

Make 24

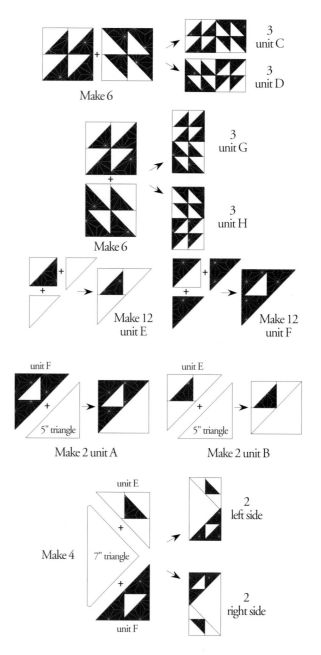

Make 6 — unit C 3 — unit D 3

Make 6 — unit G 3 — unit H 3

Make 12 unit E — Make 12 unit F

Make 2 unit A — Make 2 unit B

Make 4 — 2 left side — 2 right side

APPLIQUÉ DIRECTIONS

To make three wave squares, fold each 8" white background square on both diagonals. Finger press to mark center and fold lines. Place each square over the wave appliqué design found on page 67. Match center and diagonals. Trace wave design onto the right side of each white square.

Wave templates: Make a template for each shape #1 through #12 by tracing directly from the drawing. Note that piece #5 extends under pieces #6 and #7. Place a template on right side of light blue print fabric. Draw around the shape. Cut out with a scant ¼" seam allowance. Cut three pieces from each template #1 through #12. Cut shape #5 large enough to fit under #6 and #7.

Appliqué using the needleturn method found on pages 5-6. Use light blue matching thread. Clip to sewing lines on inside curves. Appliqué with many tiny stitches.

Pin light blue print piece #1 to background square matching line on appliqué piece to traced line on the square. Begin appliqué stitching on the outside of the curve where #1 and #2 meet. Appliqué around #1. Clip to sewing line on inside of wave curve as needed. Do not appliqué edge of #1 that is covered by #2. Repeat this procedure for piece #2.

Follow the numbered order to complete wave appliqué. Never appliqué the edge that lies under the next piece. Note that piece #5 extends under #6 and #7.

When appliqué is completed, cut away the background fabric behind the whole design. Cut appliquéd squares to 7½". Follow the diagram below to sew units E and F to appliquéd wave square. Make **three** wave units.

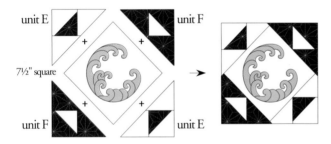

PIECING UNITS TOGETHER & FINISHING

Follow the diagram to arrange units together in three long strips. Make sure all triangles are in the correct position before you sew units together. Sew long strips together to complete quilt center. Quilt should measure 20½" x 60½" at this point.

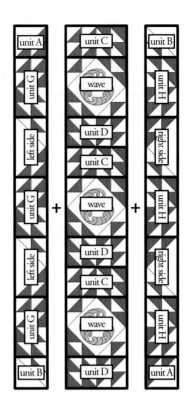

Borders: Sew two white strips 3½" x 60½" to the long sides. Sew two white strips 3½" x 26½" to the top and bottom.

Quilting Design: Quilt in the ditch around each piece of the appliquéd wave. Quilt ¼" around the outside of the wave appliqué. Quilt ¼" inside the white triangles along square corner. Do not quilt along the diagonal side. Trace and quilt wave design in white outside triangles and corner triangles.

Layer, baste, quilt, square and bind following directions on page 7-8. Don't forget to sign and date your quilt. Sew a sleeve on the back to hang your quilt.

Arabic Lattice Quilt
33" x 33"

Pieced and quilted by Teresa Reilly.

This quilt is a wonderful example of illusion. The print and solid shapes seem to hook into and interlock with each other and move in opposite directions across the quilt.

All this from only two templates! The construction is easy. The results look difficult.

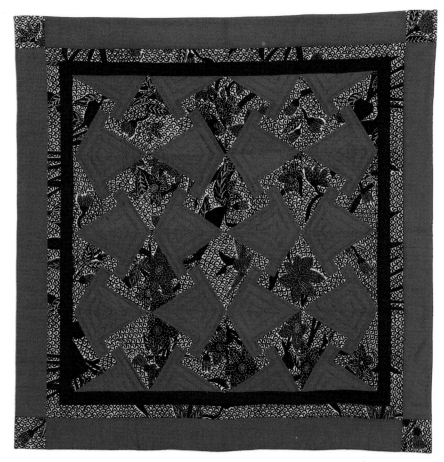

Pattern block size: 6" square

REQUIREMENTS

Fabric:
¼ yd. dark red solid
1½ yds. blue solid
1½ yds. print
1½ yds. muslin for backing and binding
batting 36" x 36"

Templates:
Template 1a, 1" square
Template 4d, page 63

CUTTING

Borders: Dark red solid
cut 2 strips 1½" x 24½"
cut 2 strips 1½" x 26½"

Borders: Print
cut 2 strips 1½" x 26½"
cut 2 strips 1½" x 28½"
cut 4 -3" squares

Borders: Blue solid
cut 4 strips 3" x 28½"

Fabric	Template 1a	Template 4d
Blue Solid	32	16 & 16r
Print	32	16 & 16r

Note: Piece 4d and 4dr (reversed) form the larger shape when the blocks are sewn together. Try to cut out patterns in fabric that fit together. Refer to the photograph of the quilt. The large blue flower has a seam in the center but appears to be a single flower.

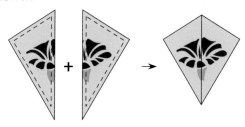

PIECING DIRECTIONS

Layout all the pieces right side up alternating A and B block arrangements. It is very important to make sure the shapes 4d and 4d reverse fabric designs fit together when blocks are sewn in rows. Recut 4d pieces if necessary.

Sew 32 print and 32 solid squares together to make 16 four patches as shown below.

Refer to the following diagrams to piece 8 blocks A and 8 blocks B.

The diagram that follows shows the piecing order to sew all the blocks together. The quilt should measure 24½" x 24½".

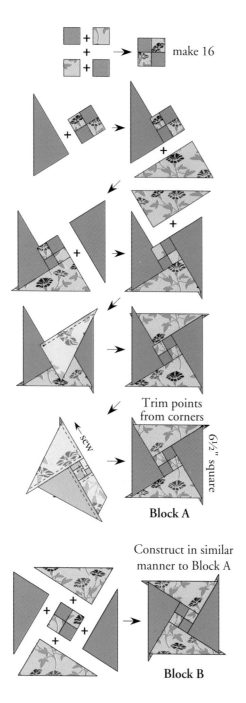

make 16

Trim points
from corners

6½" square

Block A

Construct in similar
manner to Block A

Block B

BORDERS AND QUILTING

Sew the 1½" x 24½" dark red solid strips to the top and bottom of the quilt. Sew the 1½" x 26½" dark red strips to the sides. Next sew the 1½" x 26½" print strips to the top and bottom and the 1½" x 28½" strips to the sides. Finally, sew the 3" x 28½" blue solid strips to the top and bottom. Sew a 3" square to each end of the remaining 3" x 28½" blue solid strips. Sew these strips to the sides of the quilt matching corners carefully.

Mark lines ¼" inside print shape and blue shape. The quilting diagram below shows additional lines ⅝" inside blue shape two times. Quilt around the shapes in the print fabric. Quilt in the ditch on each side of all border strips.

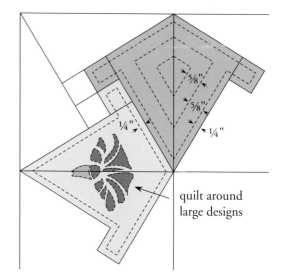

⅝"

⅝"

¼"

¼"

quilt around
large designs

Layer, baste, quilt, square and bind. Turn full width of binding to the back of the quilt. Sew sleeve on the back to hang and don't forget to sign and date your quilt.

Autumn Medallion Quilt

42" x 42"

Pieced and quilted by Teresa Reilly.

Traditional patterns are often a good source of new designs. The Joseph's Coat block has many pieces like the many colors in his coat.

I drew four blocks together and started doodling. The squares remained but many small pieces disappeared to become interwoven strips. A star formed in the center where the blocks met.

Piecing is not difficult. Sew squares, triangles, and rectangles together following the diagrams. All the pieces in this "puzzle" quilt fit together easily.

REQUIREMENTS

Fabric:

½ yd. brown floral print

¼ yd. light rust print (wave design print in quilt)

½ yd. cream print

¼ yd. cream solid

¼ yd. red print

⅛ yd. dark rust print

¼ yd. green print

½ yd. medium rust mini print

1 yd. dark brown print

1¼ yds. for backing

batting 45" x 45"

Templates:

Template 1h, 2⅛" square

Template 1g, 2¼" square*

Template 1d, 3" square*

Template 2f, 2⅛" right triangle*

Template 3f, 3" right triangle*

Template 3i, 6" right triangle**

Template 3j, 1" x 2¼" x 4¼" trapezoid

Several rectangles are cut from strips in cutting instructions.

  *   or use Easy Angle™

  **   or use Easy Angle II™

CUTTING CHART

FABRIC AND TEMPLATE NUMBER

Fabric	1h	1g	1d	2f	3f	3i	3j
Brown floral			4				20
Light rust print		12					
Cream print				56			
Cream solid				8		4	
Red print		5		24	4		
Dark rust					4		
Green print	12			8			
Medium rust mini	4						
Dark brown print	8						

ADDITIONAL CUTTING

In addition to the cutting chart above, the following also need to be cut:

Medium rust print: Cut 3 strips 2⅝" wide crossgrain. Then cut these into 8 rectangles 4¾"x 2⅝", 4 rectangles 6⅞ x 2⅝", and 4 rectangles 11⅛" x 2⅝".

Dark brown print: Cut 5 strips 2⅝" wide crossgrain. Then cut these into 8 rectangles 12"x 2⅝", and 12 rectangles 4¾" x 2⅝".

Cut 4 strips 2" wide crossgrain. Then cut these into 8 rectangles 18" x 2".

Cut 2" wide strips crossgrain. Then piece with diagonal seams to make 200" continuous strip for binding.

PIECING DIRECTIONS

Follow the diagrams to sew the pieces together to make the units as shown here:

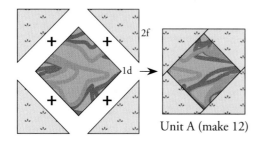

Unit A (make 12)

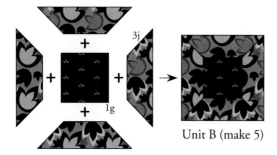

Unit B (make 5)

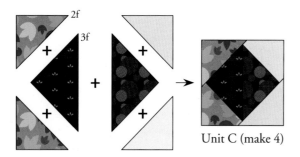

Unit C (make 4)

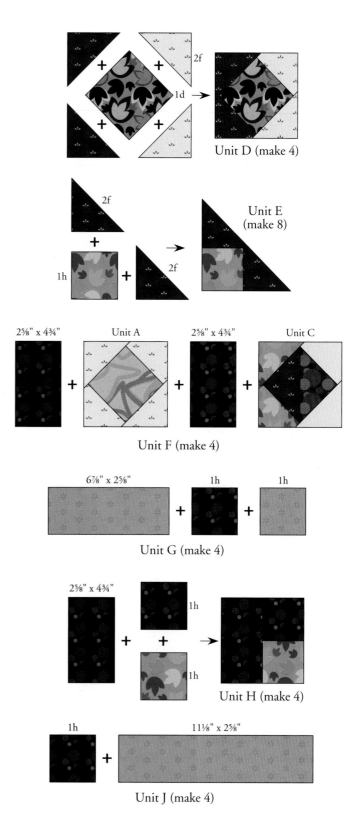

Unit D (make 4)

Unit E (make 8)

Unit F (make 4)

Unit G (make 4)

Unit H (make 4)

Unit J (make 4)

After completing the individual units, make four triangle corner units as shown here on the next page. Sew the D and E units and the rectangles together first. Then add the 3i triangle. Finally, sew the borders to the triangle corner. Pin a 2" x 18" dark brown print strip along the edge of the pieced corner. Extend the strip 2½" beyond the corner. Begin sewing ¼" in from the corner and stop ¼" from the other end. The strip will extend approximately 3½" beyond the diagonal edge.

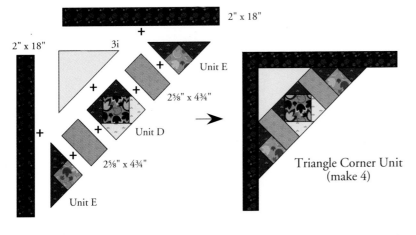

Triangle Corner Unit
(make 4)

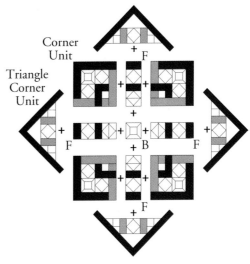

Finally sew the four triangle extensions to the sides of the quilt. Line up the rust and brown strips and squares.

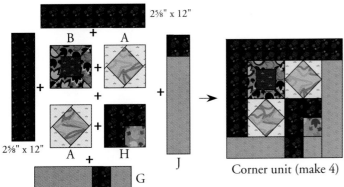

Corner unit (make 4)

Sew the strip to the other side and miter the corner following the directions on page 6.

Sew the four corner blocks together (center left illustration). Sew the A, B, and H units together. Then sew the two dark brown print 12" x 2⅝" border strips to top and side. Follow the directions for mitering the corner on page 6. Sew the G unit to the bottom. Then sew the J unit to the right side.

Follow the illustration to sew the quilt together. Sew the center part together in rows, (two rows of corner unit, F unit, and corner unit, and a row of F unit, B unit, F unit). Note that the brown rectangle in unit F must always be on the outside, and unit B must always be in the corner of the corner units. This will rotate unit J and create the interweaving of the rust and dark brown strips. The puzzle works!

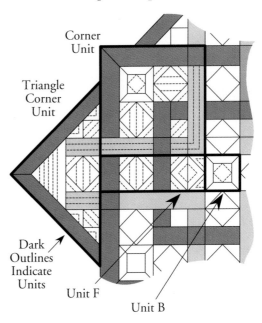

Mark quilting lines on the quilt top following the illustration above. Quilt in the ditch around all the shapes. Do not quilt on the dark brown print strips.

Layer the back, batting and quilt top. Baste following the directions on page 7.

Quilt, square, and bind the quilt following the directions on page 8. Sew a sleeve to the back for hanging. Don't forget to sign and date your quilt.

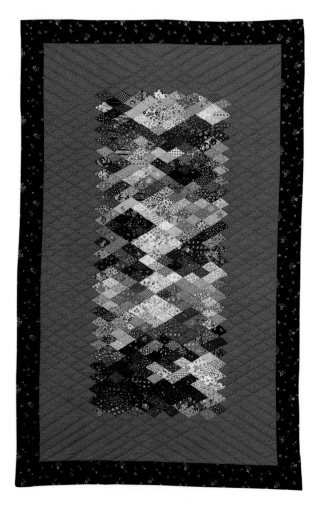

Charm Quilt
24½" x 39"

Pieced and quilted by Teresa Reilly.

A charm quilt is the ultimate scrap quilt. Every piece in the quilt must be a different fabric all cut from one pattern shape. I chose a 1" diamond. Then the fun began. I took out all my fabric and cut one diamond from each. The real challenge here was not to mix up the piles of fabric and cut the same fabric twice. I even cut diamonds from swatches I had used to order fabric by mail. Every color and fabric pattern is useful – light, medium, dark, plaid, striped, floral, mini prints, but no solids. Center a small flower in the diamond. I found a penguin who just fit. Look for him in the second row from the top.

REQUIREMENTS

Fabric:
> Scraps – 399 different fabrics
> 1 yd. solid color for background
> ½ yd. dark print for borders
> ¾ yd. for backing
> batting 28" x 42"

Templates:
> Template 1k, 1" 60° diamond

CUTTING: Use template 1k to cut 399 diamonds from your fabric collection. Use the full yard of the background for laying out the design. Cut this piece to 21" x 35½" after the center panel is pieced.

> Dark print – cut 2 strips 2½" x 26"
> Dark print – cut 2 strips 2½" x 41"
> Dark print – cut 2" wide strips crossgrain and piece with diagonal seams to make 140" continuous strip for binding.

LAYOUT AND PIECING DIRECTIONS

Sort the diamonds into light, medium and dark piles. This quilt requires 399 diamonds. I suggest that you start laying it out before cutting all 399 pieces. When the design takes shape you will soon see where more variety of color and texture is needed. I like to work on a large table so I can walk around to see the design from all sides.

Lay out the 1 yard of solid color background fabric. About 6" in from one end, place a row of 7 diamonds across the center of the fabric. Do not overlap edges. You'll be moving diamonds about as your design develops. Take 7 more pieces and make a second row. Continue adding rows until there are 57 rows.

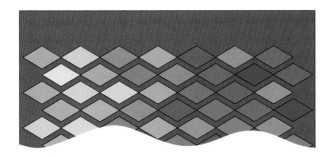

This is a random design with no repeat. You may form larger diamonds, stripes, zig-zags, etc. The most important thing to remember is that the design must please you. Walk around the table to see it from all sides. "Squint" your eyes to see color intensities. Replace dark diamonds with medium or lights. Add some darks if areas are blah with too many lights. Your eye should move across the quilt and not be stuck in any one place.

When is this quilt design finished? The answer is when you like it and decide that now is the time to sew it all together.

Sew the diamonds together in diagonal rows as shown below:

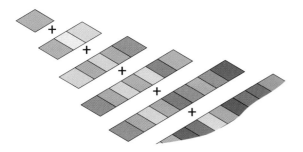

When the panel is complete, press from the right side. Be very careful not to stretch. Center this panel on the background fabric that has been cut to 21" x 35½". Pin securely and baste. The panel will be appliquéd to the background.

Instructions are found on page 5. Appliqué with a neutral color thread turning under the ¼"seam

allowance. When appliqué is complete, cut away the fabric behind the diamond panel.

Borders: Match the middle of a 2½" x 26" border strip to the middle of the quilt top so that 2½" extends beyond each edge. Sew the strips to the quilt beginning and ending ¼" from the edge. Repeat for the strip that goes on the bottom. Now sew the 2½" x 41" strips to the sides, again matching middles and starting and stopping ¼" from each edge. Miter the corners following the directions on page 6.

Mark a diamond grid on the background fabric by extending seam lines in diamond panel. Corners will have lines in one direction only. Quilt all the seam lines in the ditch through the pieced diamonds and marked grid lines. Quilt in the ditch inside the border. Do not quilt the border.

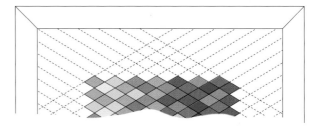

Layer, baste, quilt, square and bind following the directions on pages 7-8. Turn binding completely to back of quilt. Sew a sleeve to the back for hanging and don't forget to sign and date your quilt.

Delectable Pumpkin Mountains Quilt

49" x 49"

Appliquéd, pieced and quilted by Teresa Reilly.

Adding your variation to a traditional pattern is a "creative" challenge for quilters. Pumpkins and fall foliage always go together. My pumpkin sits in the center of the "delectable mountains" surrounded by pumpkin leaves and vines.

Pattern block size: 10" square

REQUIREMENTS

Fabric:

2 yds. beige mini print

2 yds. rust print

½ yd. dark brown/rust print

¼ yd. sage green solid

¼ yd. small green check

3 yds. for backing – pieced to make 54" square

batting 54" square

Templates:

Template 1c, 2" square

Template 3e, 2" right triangle*

8" right triangle**

*or use Easy Angle™

** or use Easy Angle II™

Appliqué: Make templates from full size drawings on page 68 and on pullout sheet for pumpkin, two pumpkin stem pieces, large and small leaves. Do not add seam allowances to templates.

Cutting Borders:

Beige mini print – cut 2 strips 2½" x 40½"

Beige mini print – cut 2 strips 2½" x 44½"

Rust print – cut 2 strips 2½" x 45½"

Rust print – cut 2 strips 2½" x 49½"

Rust print – cut 2"wide strips crossgrain and piece with diagonal seams to make 210" continuous strip for binding.

Dk. brown/rust – cut 8 strips 1" wide crossgrain. Then piece 2 strips end to end; make 4 strips; from these strips, cut 2 strips 1" x 44½" with seam in center of strip; cut 2 strips 1" x 45½" with seam in center of strip.

Cutting Pieces:

Beige mini print – cut 140 template 3e*

Beige mini print – cut 16 -8½"right triangles**

Beige mini print – cut 4 squares, template 1c

Rust print – cut 140 template 3e*

Rust print – cut 16 -8½" right triangles**

*or use Easy Angle™

** this includes ¼" seam allowance

Cutting Appliqué:

Place template on right side of fabric. Draw around template. Cut out with a scant ¼" seam allowance.

Dk brown/rust – cut 1 pumpkin

Solid green – cut 1 large pumpkin stem piece

Solid green – cut 8 small leaves

Sm. green check – cut 1 small pumpkin stem piece

Sm. green check – cut 4 large leaves

Solid green – cut ⅝" wide strip *on the bias* to equal 4 pieces 6" long; 16 pieces 3" long; 12 pieces 2" long

Piecing Directions

Sew the beige and rust small triangles together to make 140 squares. Sew the beige and rust large triangles together to make 16 squares.

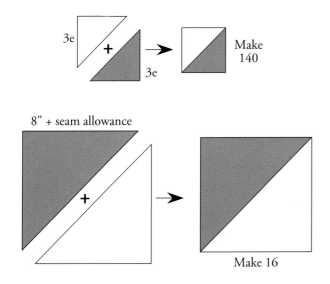

3e

+

3e

Make 140

8" + seam allowance

+

Make 16

Follow the diagrams below to make 12 squares Unit A and 4 squares Unit B.

Sew all the squares together as shown. The quilt should measure 40½" square at this point.

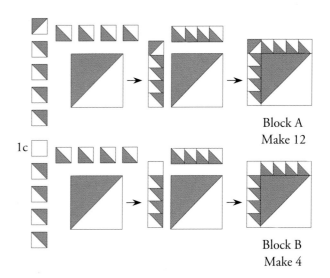

1c

Block A
Make 12

Block B
Make 4

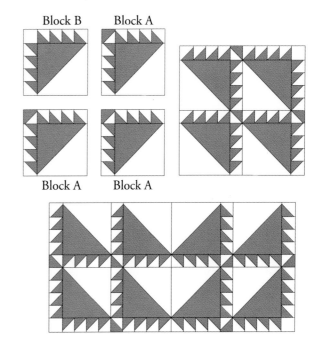

Block B   Block A

Block A   Block A

APPLIQUÉ DIRECTIONS

Pumpkin: The pumpkin is appliquéd in the center square formed by four beige triangles. Center the pumpkin template here and draw around it. Place the two stem pieces and draw around them. Pin the pumpkin appliqué piece to the beige background fabric matching the lines drawn on pumpkin to lines drawn on beige background fabric. Appliqué using needleturn method and matching dark brown thread. Use the same method to appliqué the large and then small stem pieces.

Leaves and vines: Place the large beige triangles over the drawing of two leaves and vine on page 68. Trace. "Center" mark matches the seam line.

Place the small beige triangles in the corner squares over the small leaf drawing on page 69. Trace. Match seam lines to lines at bottom of leaf drawing.

Follow this order to appliqué leaves and vines:

- short vine pieces (2" long) to make all leaf stems

- center vine pieces (6" long) for the four 2 leaf vines

- two vine pieces that extend out from sides of all leaves (3" long). Be sure to extend the vines under each other and under the leaves by ¼".

- large green check leaf and small solid green leaf in large triangle areas

- small solid green leaves in small triangles

Cut out all layers of fabric behind the appliqué pieces. Do not cut out behind vines.

BORDERS AND QUILTING DIRECTIONS

Sew the 2½" x 40½" beige background strips to top and bottom of quilt. Then sew the 2½" x 44½" beige background fabric strips to each side.

Sew the 1" x 44½" dark brown/rust strips to the top and bottom. Then sew the 1" x 45½" dark brown/rust strips to each side.

Sew the 2½" x 45½" rust print fabric strips to the top and bottom. Then sew the 2½" x 49½" rust print fabric strips to each side.

Quilt in the ditch around all the appliquéd shapes. Quilt in the ditch on both sides of the narrow dark brown border. Mark and quilt vein lines in leaves and pumpkins.

Follow the diagram below to mark straight lines from center to edge of narrow border.

Each quarter of the quilt will have lines radiating from the center. Quilt across large rust triangles. Do not quilt across appliqué.

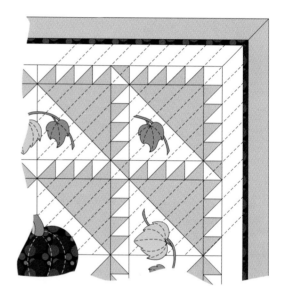

Layer the back, batting and quilt top. Baste following the directions on page 7. Quilt, square and bind. Sew sleeve on the back of quilt for hanging. Don't forget to sign and date your quilt.

Plaid Bear's Paw Quilt

32½" x 32½"

Pieced and quilted by Teresa Reilly.

Here in New England we call this pattern Bear's Paw. You may have heard it called Duck's Foot in the Mud if you live where there are more ducks than bears. The plaid fabric for my quilt was left over from making shirts for my three sons. I had originally planned for plaid strips to separate the four blocks. But as often happens when using scraps, the quilt changes when you run out of fabric. What a great surprise to find a "star" in the center where the blocks come together.

Pattern block size: 14" square

REQUIREMENTS

Fabric:
  1 yd. plaid
  ½ yd. small yellow print
  ¾ yd. muslin
  ½ yd. red solid
  1 yd. for backing
  batting 36" square

Templates:
  Template 1c, 2" square
  Template 3e, 2" right triangle*
  Template 1e, 4" square
  Template 3b, 2" x 6" rectangle
  *or use Easy Angle™

CUTTING DIRECTIONS

Cut border strips from plaid fabric so that lines or pattern in plaid frames the quilt. The plaid triangles can be cut without attention to pattern.

CUTTING CHART FOR TEMPLATES

Fabric	1c	1e	3b	3e
Plaid	4			64
Yellow		16		
Muslin	16		16	64

Before cutting the pieces from the chart above, the following strips must be cut:

Plaid – cut 4 strips 2½" x 34" for borders

Red – cut 4 strips 1" x 34" for border

Red – cut 2" wide strips crossgrain. Then piece with diagonal seams to make 142" continuous strip for binding.

PIECING DIRECTIONS

Sew plaid and muslin triangles together to make 64 squares. Follow the diagram below to sew the units together.

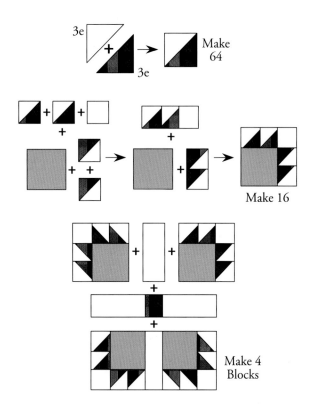

Sew the four completed blocks together. The quilt should measure 28½" x 28½" at this point.

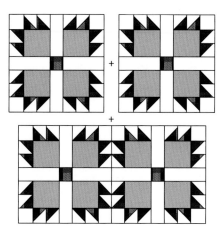

BORDERS, QUILTING AND FINISHING DIRECTIONS

Borders: Sew the red and plaid border strips together lengthwise. Match the center of this border strip to center point on the side of the quilt with red fabric next to the quilt. Sew the border to the quilt beginning and ending ¼" from each end. Add borders to the three other sides. Border pieces extend beyond the corners of the quilt. Miter the corners following the directions on page 6.

Quilting: Follow the diagram to mark the quilting lines. Quilt in the ditch on both sides of the narrow red border. Quilt the plaid lines in the center of the border.

Layer the back, batting, and quilt top. Baste together, then quilt, square and bind. Sew a sleeve to the back for hanging. Don't forget to sign and date your quilt.

Schoolhouse Quilt
48" x 60"

Pieced and quilted by Teresa Reilly.

Quilters started piecing the schoolhouse block back in 1910. It is still a favorite. I combined it with a winged 9-patch block. The center star from this block makes an interesting corner in the borders.

Pattern block size: 12" schoolhouse
                      12" winged 9-patch

REQUIREMENTS

Fabric:

3 yds. dark red print for border, schoolhouse and patches
1½ yds. medium print
2½ yds. light cream solid
4 yds. for backing
batting 54" x 66"

Templates:

Schoolhouse – full size A through N on pullout
2" x 8" rectangle
2" x 12" rectangle
Winged 9-patch
Template 1b, 1½" square
Template 1d, 3" square
Template 2e, 1½" right triangle
Template 4a, triangle with 3" base and 1½" height

SCHOOLHOUSE CUTTING CHART

Fabric	A	B	C	D	E	F	G	H	Hr	I	J	K	L	M	N
Dk red	6	6	12	12	12	6	12								
Lt cream solid								6	6	6	6	6	6	6	12

WINGED 9-PATCH CUTTING CHART

Fabric	1b	1d	2e	4a
Dark red	72			88
Med print	72			24
Lt cream solid	72	10	80	24

Before following the cutting charts shown here, additional strips must be cut.

CUTTING BORDERS: Cut all borders lengthwise of fabric.

> Dark red print – cut 2 strips 3½" x 48½" for center side borders
>
> Dark red print – cut 2 strips 3½" x 36½" for top and bottom center borders
>
> Dark red print – cut 2" wide strips crossgrain. Then piece with diagonal seams to equal 240" continuous strip for binding.
>
> Medium print – cut 2 strips 2" x 48½" for outer side borders
>
> Medium print – cut 2 strips 2" x 36½" for outer top and bottom borders
>
> Light cream solid – cut 2 strips 2" x 48½" for inner side borders
>
> Light cream solid – cut 2 strips 2" x 36½" for inner top and bottom borders

CUTTING SCHOOLHOUSE:

> Light cream solid – cut 12 pieces 2½" x 8½" for top and bottom of blocks
>
> Light cream solid – cut 12 pieces 2½" x 12½" for sides of blocks

PIECING DIRECTIONS

Schoolhouse block: Make templates A through N from the template diagram. The templates are for marking sewing lines. You must add ¼" seam allowance when cutting fabric. Follow cutting chart.

Winged 9-patch block: Follow the piecing diagram below to make the winged 9-patch blocks.

Make 24 Unit A. Make 24 Unit B. Cut 10 Unit C. Make 4 star units for the border.

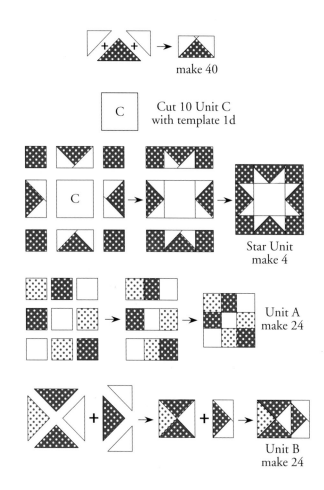

make 40

Cut 10 Unit C with template 1d

Star Unit make 4

Unit A make 24

Unit B make 24

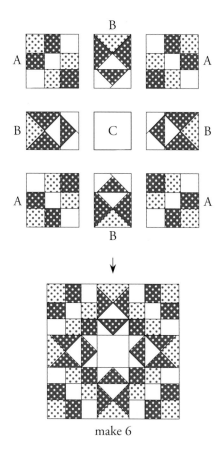

make 6

Follow the sequence below to piece the schoolhouse blocks:

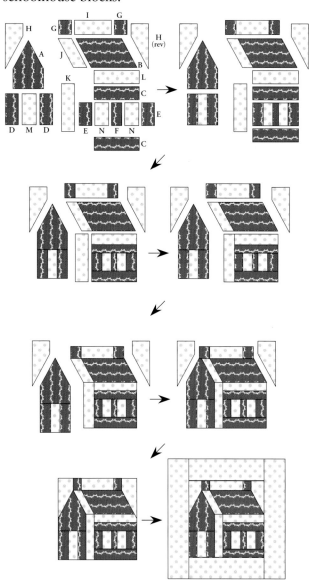

Sew 2½" x 8½" rectangles to the top and bottom of each pieced schoolhouse. Sew 2½" x 12½" rectangles to each side of the schoolhouse blocks. All completed blocks are 12½" x 12½".

Follow the diagram to sew the blocks together. The quilt should measure 36½" x 48½" at this point.

Sew the side border strips together – medium print to dark red to light cream solid. Make two sets. Then sew these to the sides of the quilt top. Sew the top and bottom border strips together – medium print to dark red to light cream solid. Make two sets. Then sew a star block to each end of the strip sets. Sew the top and bottom borders to the quilt.

QUILTING DESIGNS AND FINISHING

Mark quilting lines ¼" outside the dark red print shapes of the schoolhouses. Follow the quilting diagrams below for the winged 9-patch blocks. Note how the lines extend into the background areas of the schoolhouse blocks.

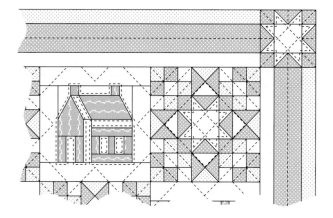

Quilt in the ditch on both sides of the border strips and in the center of the dark red print strip.

Layer the back, batting and top. Baste following directions on page 7. Quilt, square and bind.

Don't forget to sign and date your quilt.

Christmas Basket Quilt

26" x 26"

Appliquéd, pieced and quilted by Teresa Reilly.

Basket quilts are made from many patterns in every season. My basket is pieced from Christmas fabrics. Adding holly leaves and berries to the handles and borders complete this holiday wall quilt.

Pattern block size: 12" basket square set on point making a 17" square when corner triangles are added.

REQUIREMENTS

Fabric:
½ yd. light print for background
1 yd. red print
⅛ yd. red floral print
⅛ yd. red pin dot
¼ yd. green floral print
¼ yd. green pin dot (gold dots)
¼ yd. green solid
1 yd. for backing
batting 30" x 30" square

Templates:
Template 1c, 2" square

Template 3e*, 2" right triangle
Template 3g*, 4" right triangle
8½" right triangle**
12" right triangle
Template 2h, page 61
Templates for handle shape, large and small
    holly leaves, large and small holly berries,
    page 69
*or use Easy Angle™; **or use Easy Angle II™

FABRIC AND TEMPLATE CUTTING CHART

Fabric	1c	2h	2hr	3e	3g	8½"triangle	12" triangle
Light print		1	1		1	4	1
Red floral	1			5		add ¼" seam allowances when	
Green floral				11		cutting these triangles	

Before cutting these pieces, additional strips must be cut for borders.

CUTTING BORDERS:
Red print – cut 2 strips 4½" x 19"
Red print – cut 2 strips 4½" x 27"
Red print – cut 2" wide strips crossgrain and
    piece with diagonal seams to equal 120"
    continuous strip for binding.
Green pin dot – cut 2 strips 1¼" x 17½"
Green pin dot – cut 2 strips 1¼" x 19"

CUTTING APPLIQUÉ: Place template on right side of fabric. Draw around template and cut out with scant ¼" seam allowance.
Green pin dot – cut 12 large holly leaves
Green pin dot – cut 4 small holly leaves
Green solid – cut 10 large holly leaves
Green solid – cut 7 small holly leaves
Green floral – cut 1 strip 1¼" wide x 21" long
    on the bias
Red pin dot – cut 6 large holly berries
Red pin dot – cut 3 small holly berries

PIECING & APPLIQUÉ DIRECTIONS

Sew red and green triangles together to make five squares. Follow the diagram below to piece the basket:

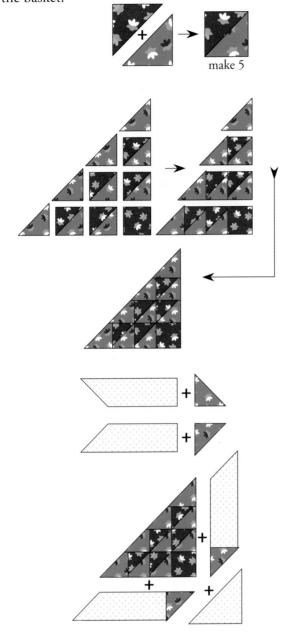

make 5

Basket Handle: Center the handle template on the right side of the 12½" triangle of the background fabric. Then draw around the template.

On the right side of the bias cut handle strip, draw a ¼" seam line on both lengthwise edges. Place bias handle strip over the drawn handle matching the center of the strip to the center of the drawn handle. Pin in place.

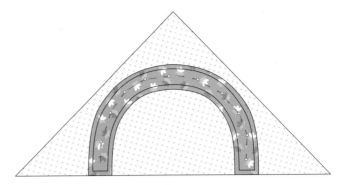

On the inside curve of the bias strip tuck under the ¼" seam allowance matching lines on the bias strip to the line drawn on the background fabric. Pin from center towards the left end of the handle to hold turned edge evenly. Use lots of pins! Do not stretch!

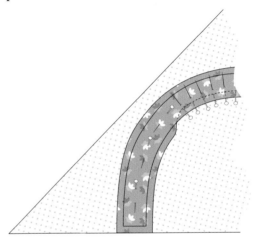

Appliqué with matching green thread. Begin in the center and appliqué towards the left end. Remove pins as you sew. Repeat these steps to turn under and appliqué the inside curve from center to right end of handle. Now turn under ¼" on the outside curve. Match the line on the handle and line drawn on the background. Appliqué this edge.

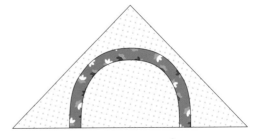

Sew handle triangle to basket triangle completing the basket square. Sew the diagonal edge of the 8½" triangles to the sides of the basket square.

Your completed square is 17½" at this point. Trim square if necessary.

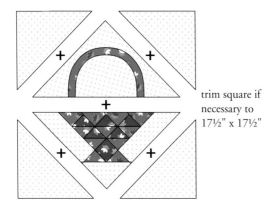

trim square if necessary to 17½" x 17½"

Borders: Sew a 1¼" x 17½" green pin dot strip to top and bottom. Sew a 1¼" x 19" green pin dot strip to each side. Sew a 4½" x 19" red print strip to top and bottom. Sew a 4½" x 27" red print strip to each side.

Holly leaves and berries: Follow the diagram below to place two green pin dot and 3 solid green small holly leaves on the basket handle. Pin and appliqué each leaf in order of 1-5. Use needleturn method and green matching thread.

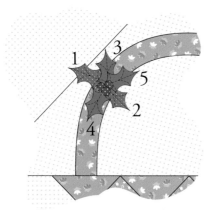

Prepare 3 small red pin dot berries using paper piecing method. See instructions for circles on page 6. Appliqué berries in center of holly leaves using red matching thread.

Follow the diagram that follows to place holly leaves and berries in upper right and lower left corners and borders. Start in the center with green pin dot leaf. Alternate with solid green leaves overlapping randomly. Place one large solid green leaf in corner diagonally with the tip extending into the light background square. One small pin

dot and two small solid green leaves fill the outer corner. Pin and appliqué each leaf in order of 1-9. Use needleturn method and green matching thread.

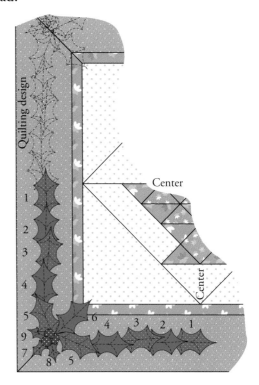

Prepare six large red pin dot berries using paper piecing methods. Appliqué berries in center of corner holly leaves using red matching thread.

When all appliqué is complete cut out all layers of fabric behind the appliqué pieces. Remove paper circles from appliquéd berries.

QUILTING DESIGNS AND FINISHING

Mark diagonal lines 1" apart across the background square. Do not draw across the basket and handle.

Quilt in the ditch around the basket pieces and handle, and around all holly leaves and berries. Quilt ¼" inside triangles and square basket pieces. Quilt vein lines in holly leaves.

Use template for holly leaves to mark quilting lines in upper left and lower right corners and borders to duplicate the appliquéd borders.

Layer the back, batting and top of the quilt. Baste together following directions on page 7. Quilt, square and bind. Don't forget to sign and date your quilt.

Double Irish Chain Quilt

46" x 46"

Pieced and quilted by Teresa Reilly.

One of the oldest patterns, this perennial favorite is made with enthusiasm by many beginning quilters. My Double Irish Chain is ready for visiting grandchildren.

REQUIREMENTS

Fabric:
1½ yds. small red print
¾ yd. green print
3 yds. white
batting 52" x 52" square

Templates:
Template 1c, 2" square
Template 3b, 2" x 6" rectangle

CUTTING CHART
FABRIC AND TEMPLATE NUMBER

Fabric	1c	3b
Red print	72	
Green print	128	
White	32	16

Before cutting pieces from the chart these strips must be cut:

Red print – cut 2 strips 3¼" x 40½" lengthwise

Red print – cut 2 strips 3¼" x 46½" lengthwise

Red print – 2" wide strips lengthwise of fabric. Then piece with diagonal seams to make 200" continuous strip for binding.

White – cut 1 strip 26½" x 104". Cut this strip in half to equal two pieces 52" long. Sew the long sides together to make a piece 52" x 52".

White – cut 8 rectangles 6½" x 10½"

PIECING DIRECTIONS

Follow the diagram below to piece red, green and white squares to make 16 of row 1, 16 of row 2, 8 of row 3, and 16 of row 4.

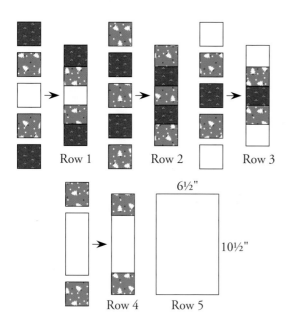

Use row 1, 2 and 3 to piece eight of Block A.

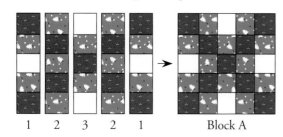

Use row 4 and 5 to piece eight of Block B.

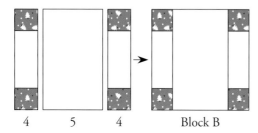

Follow the diagram below to piece Blocks A and B together.

Quilt should measure 40½" x 40½" at this point.

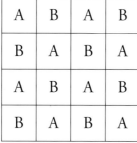

A	B	A	B
B	A	B	A
A	B	A	B
B	A	B	A

BORDERS, QUILTING AND FINISHING

Sew a 3¼" x 40½" red print strip to the top and bottom of the quilt. Sew a 3¼" x 46½" red print strip to each side of the quilt.

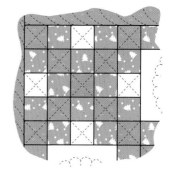

Mark diagonal lines in both directions through all the red print squares and white squares in Block A as shown.

Do not quilt in the green print squares.

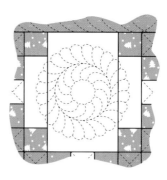

Copy the feather wreath quilting design found on the pullout sheet. Go over all the lines with black pen. Center the pattern under white Block B and trace onto the quilt top.

Copy the feather border quilting design found on the pullout sheet. Go over all the lines with black pen. Place pattern under a corner of the red border. Place inside straight line on seam line. Trace onto quilt top. Move pattern and trace feathers, stopping at the center of the border. Now place the pattern under the adjacent corner and trace. Feathers will meet in the center and form a heart.

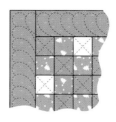 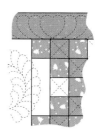

Layer the back, batting and quilt top. Baste following directions on page 7. Quilt, square and bind. Sew sleeve on the back and don't forget to sign and date your quilt.

Feathered Star Christmas Quilt

21½" x 51½"

Pieced and quilted by Teresa Reilly.

Feathered stars are not difficult to piece. Just follow the step-by-step directions to successfully piece this pattern. Use red and green fabrics to make a winter holidays feathered star.

Pattern block size: 15" feathered star

REQUIREMENTS

Fabric:

½ yd. dark red solid
¼ yd. dark red print
⅛ yd. medium red print
1 yd. dark green print
1 yd. beige mini print
1½ yds. backing
batting 28" x 54"

Templates:

Template 1a, 1" square
Template 3d, 1" right triangle
Template S2, 1¼" right triangle
Template S4, 1⅜" diamond
Template 1j, 4⅜" square
Template 4e, 4⅜" right triangle
Templates S1, S2, S3, S4,
    page 70.

CUTTING CHART – FABRIC AND TEMPLATE NUMBER

Fabric	1a	3d	S2	S4	1j	4e	S1	S3
Dk. red print								16
Md. red print								8
Dk. red solid					24		**3**	
Dk. gr. print	24	96						
Beige mini		144	24		12	12		

CUTTING DIRECTIONS BORDERS

Before cutting the pieces from the cutting chart, the following pieces must be cut:

Dark green print – cut 5 strips 3" wide crossgrain. From one strip cut 2 pieces 3" x 16½". Piece remaining strips to make 2 strips 3" x 51½" long with the seam in the center of the strips.

Dark green print – cut 2" wide strips crossgrain. Piece with diagonal seams to make 160" continuous strip for binding.

Dark red solid – cut 5 strips 1" wide crossgrain. From 1 strip cut two pieces 1" x 15½". Piece remaining strips to make 2 strips 1" x 46½" long with seam in the center of strip.

PIECING DIRECTIONS

Sew 4 beige triangles S2 to the corners of the red center to make Unit 1 as shown below:

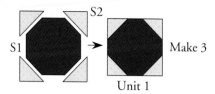

Unit 1

Sew green print and beige mini print triangles together to make 96 squares as shown.

Follow the diagram below to piece the "feather" strips A, B, C and D. Make 12 of each "feather" strip.

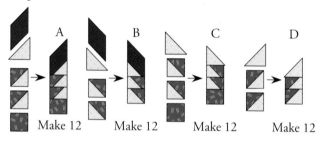

Follow the diagram below to sew strips A and B to the corner beige square to make 12 of Unit 2.

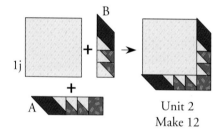

Unit 2
Make 12

Construct Unit 3 following the diagram below. Sew a dark red S3 piece to a beige S2 triangle. Sew strip C to a dark red print piece S3. Add strip D, then the S3 – S2 pieces to complete the unit. Make 8 units with dark red print fabric S3 and 4 units with medium red print fabric S3.

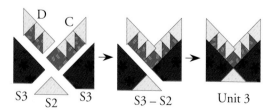

Follow the diagram below to piece the units together in rows to make 3 stars(one with medium red print S3 pieces). Set in beige print triangles 4e last to complete the square. Sew star squares in a row placing medium red print star in the middle.

Quilt should measure 12½" x 36½" at this point.

BORDERS, QUILTING AND FINISHING

Sew a 1" x 15½" dark red solid strip to the top and bottom of the quilt. Sew a 1" x 46½" dark red solid strip to each side of the quilt. Sew a 3" x 16½" dark green print strip to the top and bottom of the quilt. Sew a 3" x 51½" dark green print strip to each side.

Follow the diagram to mark and quilt the beige background areas. See the quilting diagram on page 70 to mark and quilt the red center of each star.

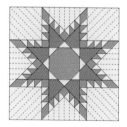

Quilt in the ditch around all the shapes in the star. Quilt in the ditch on both sides of the dark red border.

Layer, baste, quilt, square and bind. See instructions on page 7-8. Sew a sleeve on the back and don't forget to sign and date your quilt.

Holiday Mariner's Compass Quilt
21" x 45"

Pieced and quilted by Teresa Reilly.

Don't be afraid of this pattern. All these points are really pieced as straight lines. The completed circle is appliquéd to a square of the same fabric so all points are perfect!

Pattern block size: 12" square

REQUIREMENTS

Fabric:

1 yd. dark green print
1 yd. yellow solid
¼ yd. dark red solid
⅛ yd. gold lamé with fabric backing
⅛ yd. green lamé with fabric backing
¼ yd. green solid
¼ yd. dark red print
¼ yd. red floral print (If you want to place circle and piece #8 in separate patterns buy more fabric.)
1½ yds. backing
batting 27" x 51"

Templates:

Templates 1 through 8, page 71.
Make a cutting line template and a sewing line template for each pattern piece. Trace the large template on wrong side of fabric. Center small template and mark sewing line before cutting out pieces. Carefully follow the arrows on template to place on the straight of fabric.

CUTTING CHART - FABRIC AND TEMPLATE NUMBER

Fabric	1	2	3	4	5	6	7	8
Yellow solid	96							
Dk. green print		48						
Dk. green solid				24				
Dk red print							12	
Red floral						12		3
Gold lamé					24			
Green lamé			48					

CUTTING DIRECTIONS BORDERS

Before cutting the pieces from the cutting chart, the following pieces must be cut:

Dk. green print – cut 2 strips 3¼" x 21"
Dk. green print – cut 2 strips 3¼" x 39½".

Dk. green print – cut 2" wide strips cross-grain. Piece with diagonal seams to make 142" continuous strip for binding.
Dk. red solid – cut 2 strips 1½" x 12½"
Dk. red solid – cut 2 strips 1½" x 38½"
Yellow solid – cut 2 strips 1" x 14½"
Yellow solid – cut 2 strips 1" x 39½"
Yellow solid – cut 3 squares 13" x 13"

The compass is pieced from the outside creating wedges. Pieces are sewn together with straight seams to make larger wedges. The center circle is appliquéd. The completed compass is appliquéd to a background square. All these many points are formed by sewing straight seams. Be accurate!! Match sewing lines and sew very accurately.

Sew green lamé piece #3 to dark green print piece #2. Make 48 as shown below:

Sew gold lamé piece #5 to dark green solid piece #4. Make 48 as shown below:

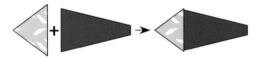

Sew a yellow piece #1 to each side of green print/green lamé piece. Wedge A is now complete. Make 48 as shown below:

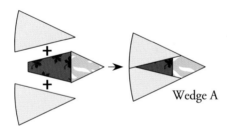

Sew wedge A to each side of dark green solid/gold lamé piece. Wedge B is now complete. Make 24 as shown:

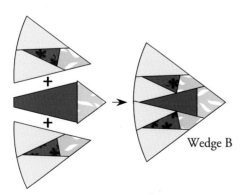

Sew wedge B to each side of red floral piece #6. Wedge C is now complete. Make 12 as shown:

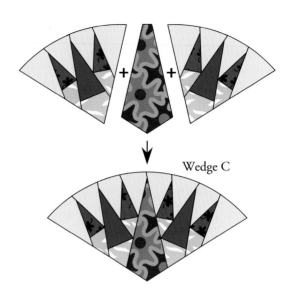

Sew one side of dark red print piece #7 to the right side of wedge C. Wedge D is now complete. Make 12 as shown below:

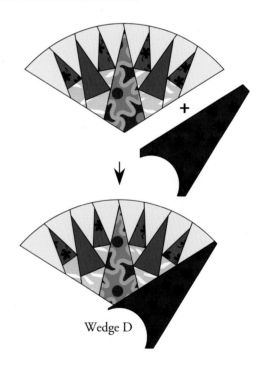

~ 58 ~

Sew four wedge D together to complete the compass as shown. Make three compasses.

Center circle: Cut three paper templates from #8 sewing line. Center and pin paper template on wrong side of floral fabric circle. Turn seam allowance over edge of paper and baste fabric to paper. Before appliquéing center circle, gently press pieced compass. All seam allowances are pressed away from the points. Be very careful not to stretch. Follow instructions on page 6 and appliqué the center circle using matching thread. Remove basting stitches and paper.

Center the completed compass on 13" yellow fabric square. Baste 1" inside the edge of the compass to hold securely. Turn under ¼" seam allowance and appliqué using matching yellow thread.

Cut background fabric away behind compass leaving ¼" seam allowance. Clip this seam allowance and press this seam and compass seam allowance away from the center. All the points will be sharp! Cut each completed square to 12½" x 12½". Sew the squares together in a row. Quilt should measure 12½" x 36½" at this point.

BORDERS, QUILTING AND FINISHING

Borders: Sew a 1½" x 12½" dark red solid strip to the top and bottom of the quilt. Sew a 1½" x 38½" dark red solid to each side.

Sew a 1" x 14½" yellow solid strip to the top and bottom. Then sew 1" x 39½" yellow strips to each side.

Sew a 3¼" x 39½" dark green print strip to each side. Sew a 3¼" x 21" dark green print strip to the top and bottom of the quilt.

Quilting: Draw straight lines from the compass points to the edge of the square. Lines will meet where squares are seamed together as shown below:

Quilt in the ditch around all the pieces in the Mariner's compass. Do not quilt the seam where the compass is appliquéd to the background square. Quilt in the ditch on both sides of the dark red and yellow border strips.

Layer the back, batting and quilt top. Baste following directions on page 7. Quilt, square and bind. Sew sleeve to the back of the quilt for hanging. Don't forget to sign and date your quilt.

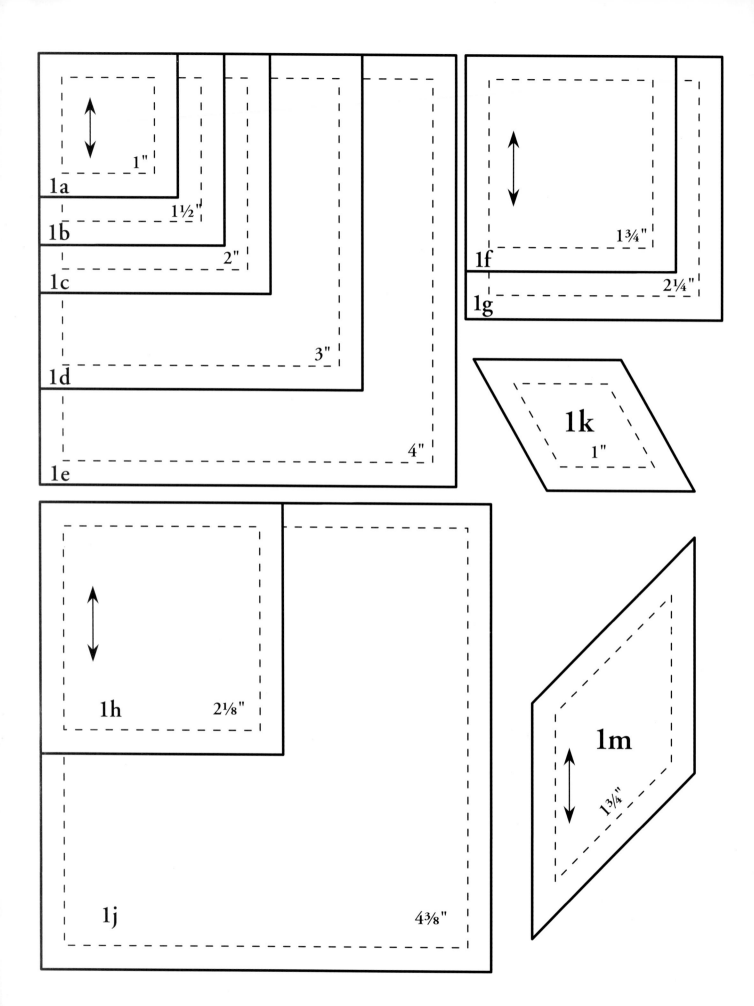

1a

1"

1b

1½"

1c

2"

1d

3"

1e

4"

1f

1¾"

1g

2¼"

1k

1"

1h

2⅛"

1j

4⅜"

1m

1¾"

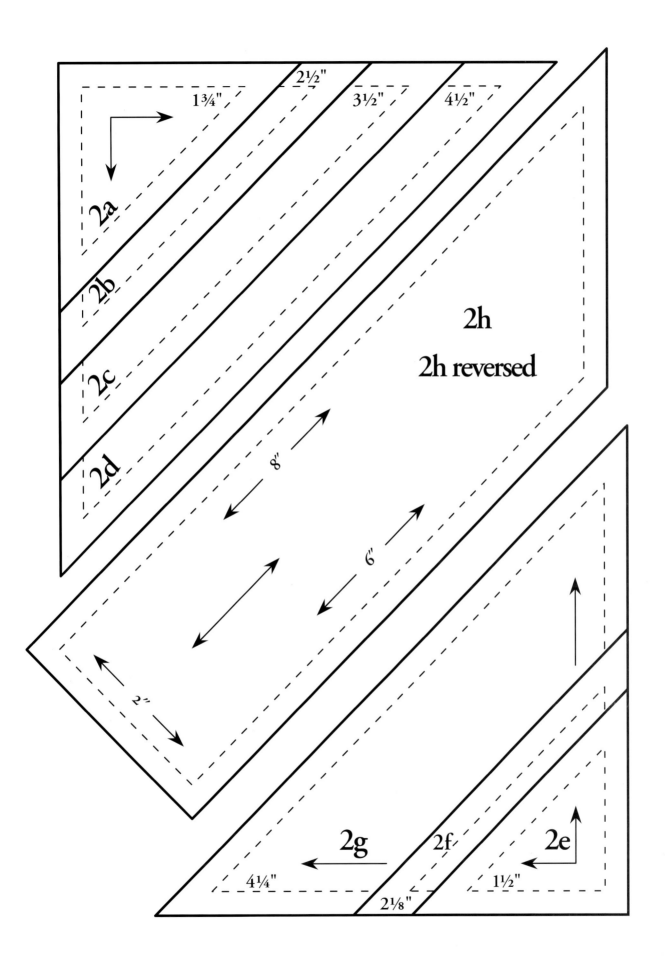

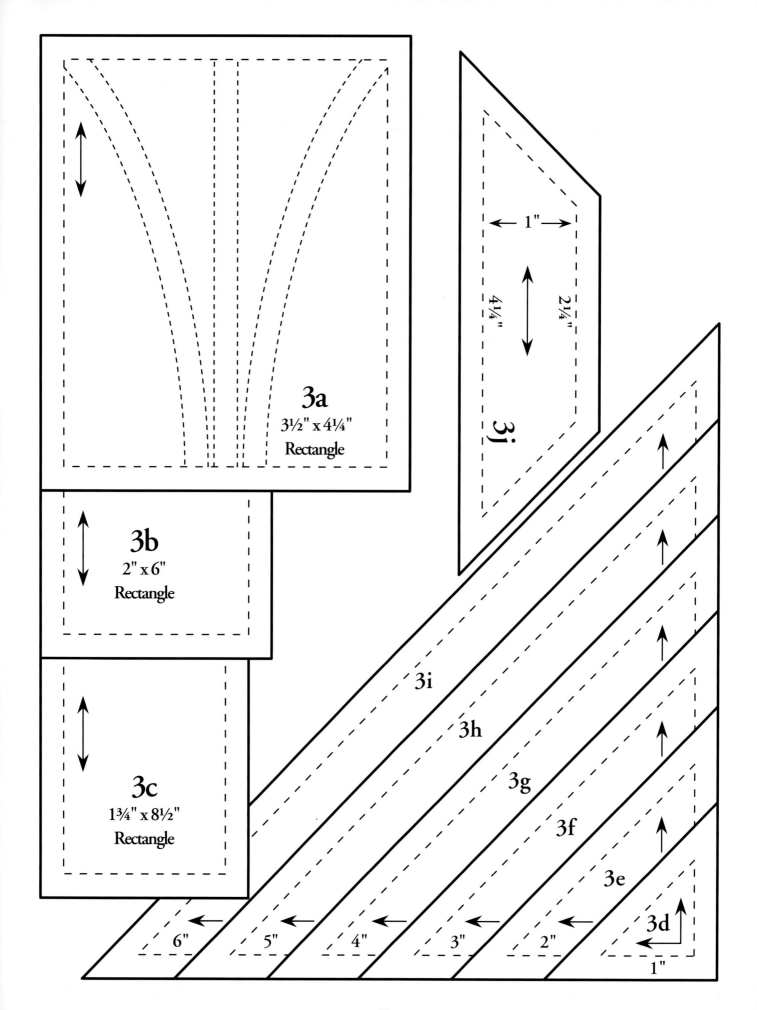

3a
3½" x 4¼"
Rectangle

3b
2" x 6"
Rectangle

3c
1¾" x 8½"
Rectangle

3j
1"
4¼"
2¼"

3i
3h
3g
3f
3e
3d

6"   5"   4"   3"   2"   1"

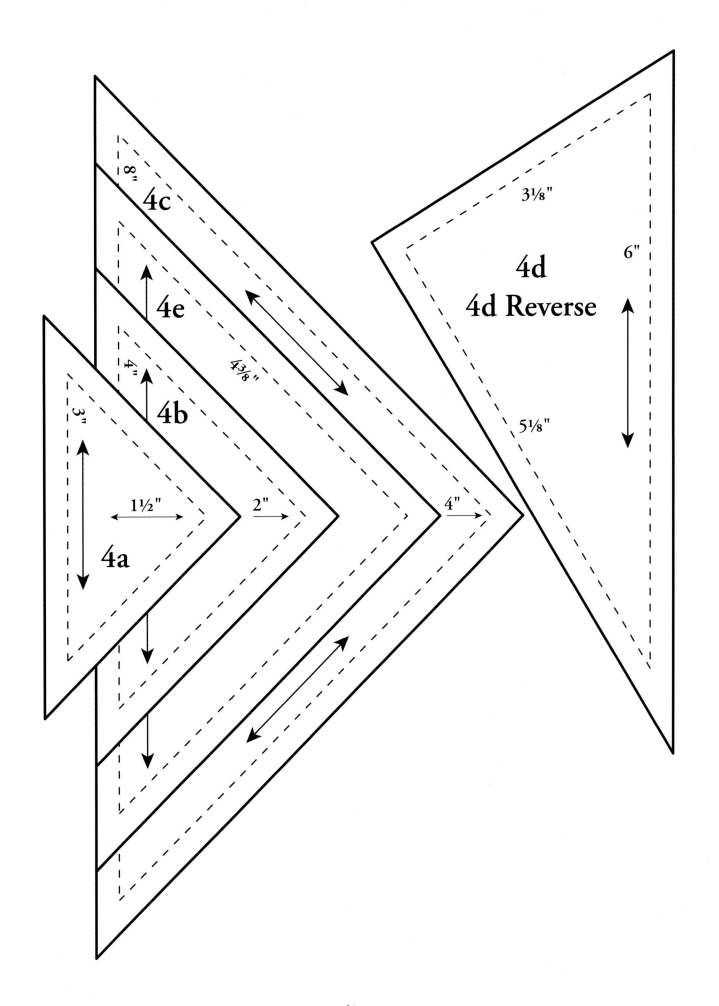

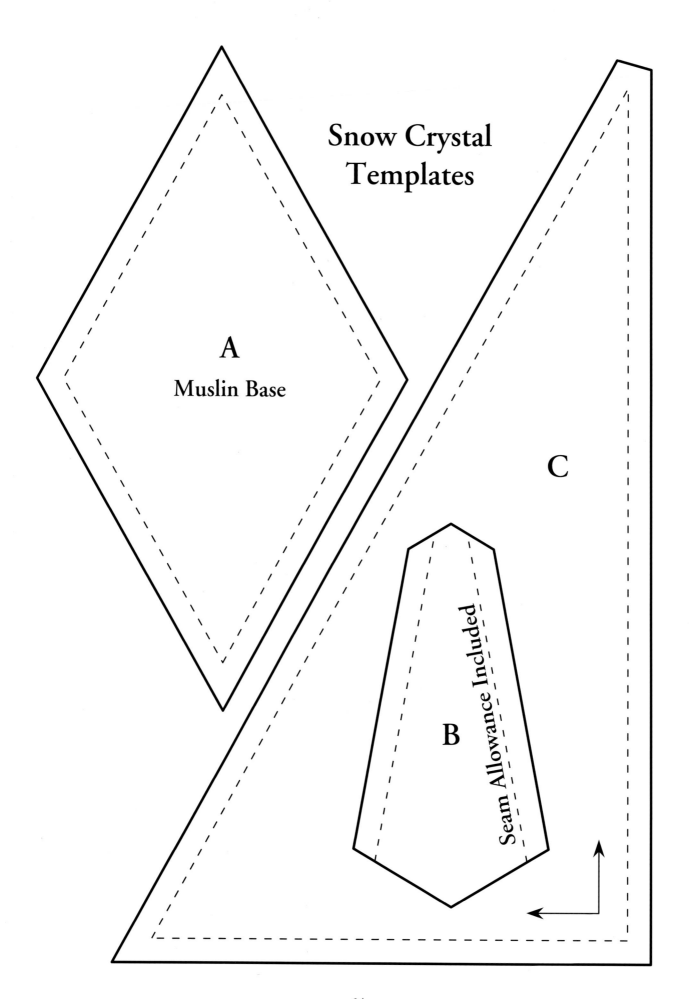

Snow Crystal
Templates

A

Muslin Base

C

B

Seam Allowance Included

Pineapple Log Cabin Templates
Add ¼" Seam Allowance

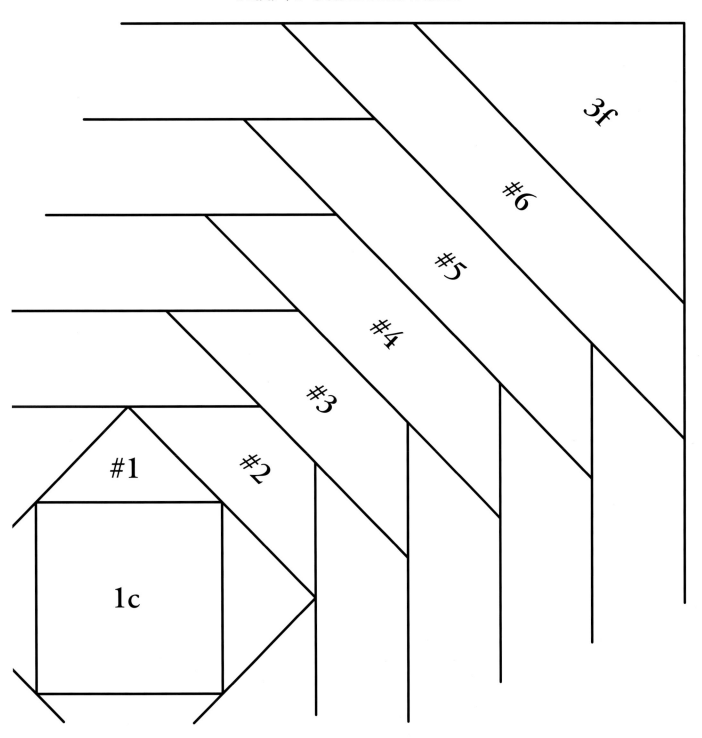

3f

#6

#5

#4

#3

#1

#2

1c

Pineapple
Appliqué Design

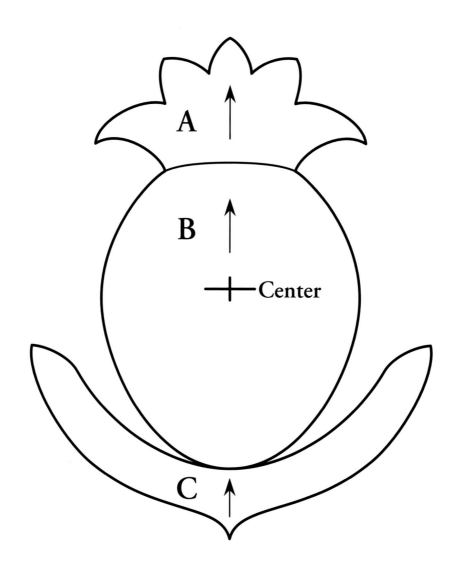

Ocean Waves Appliqué and Large Templates

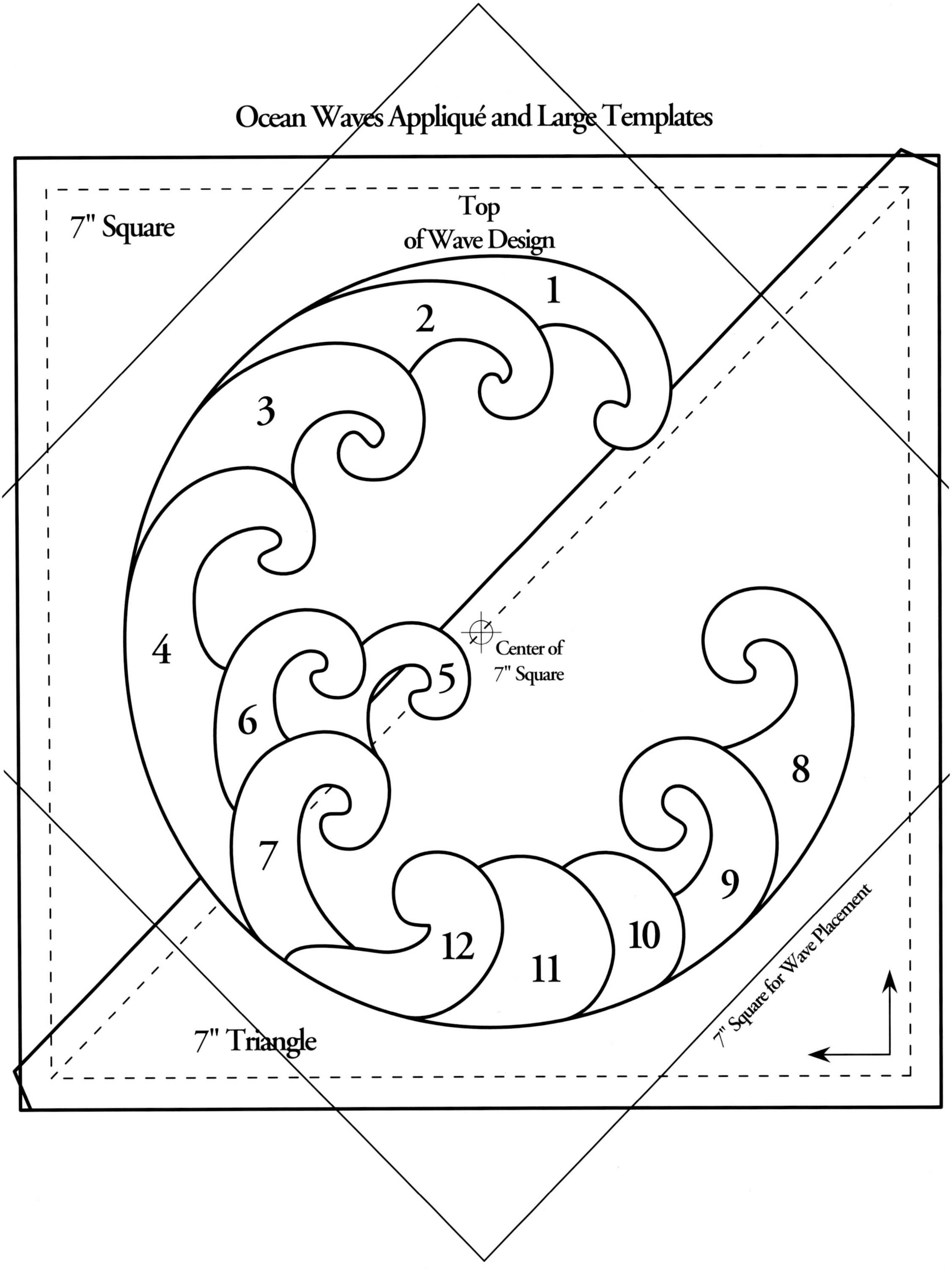

7" Square

Top
of Wave Design

1

2

3

4

5

6

7

8

9

10

11

12

Center of
7" Square

7" Triangle

7" Square for Wave Placement

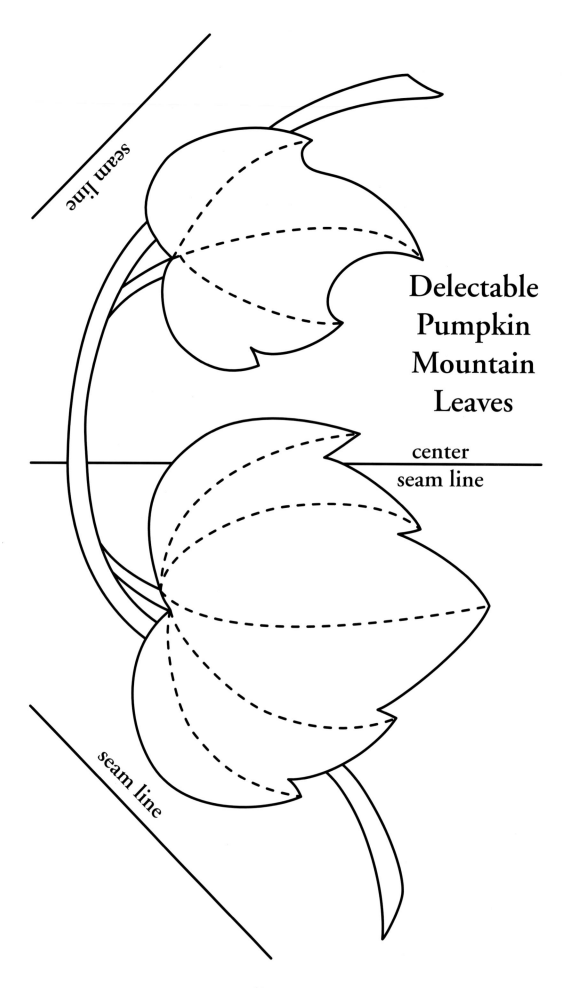

seam line

Delectable
Pumpkin
Mountain
Leaves

center
seam line

seam line

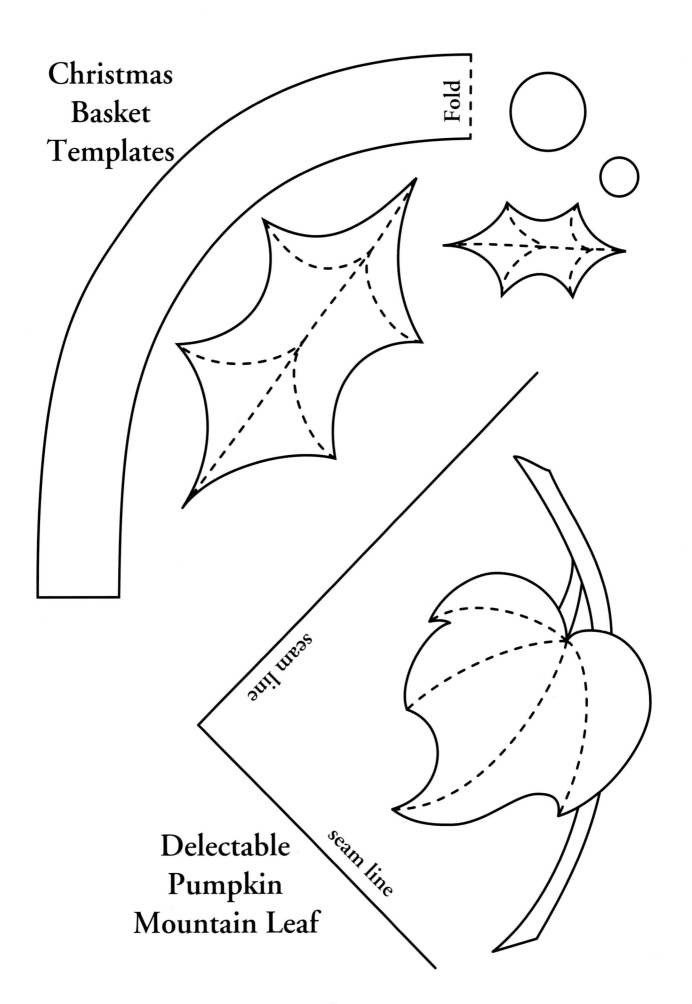

Christmas
Basket
Templates

Fold

seam line

seam line

Delectable
Pumpkin
Mountain Leaf

Feathered Star
Templates

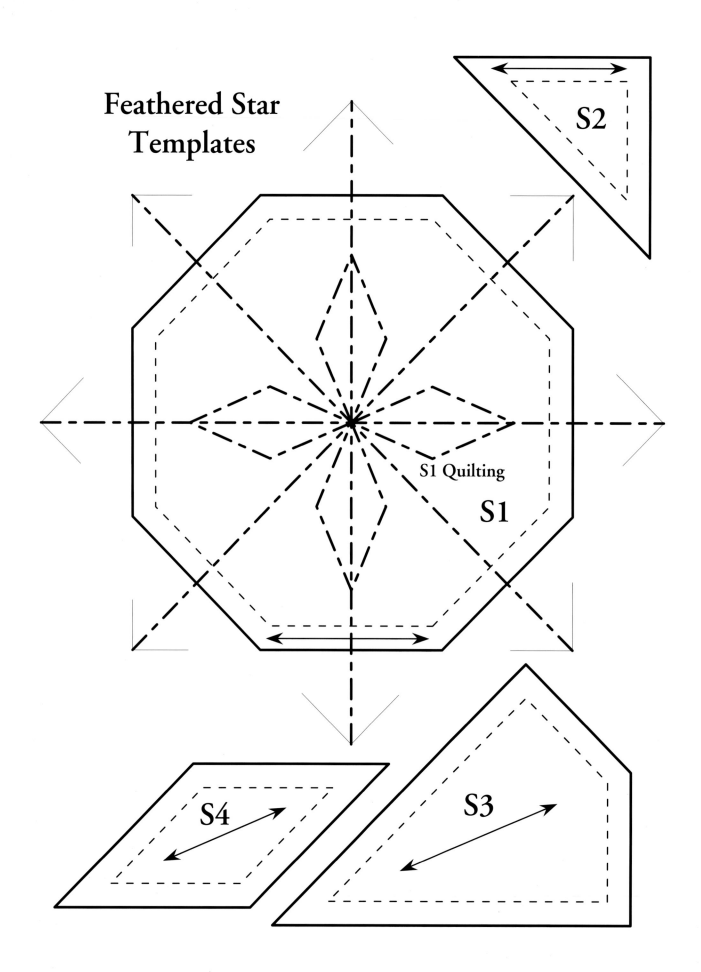

S2

S1 Quilting

S1

S4

S3

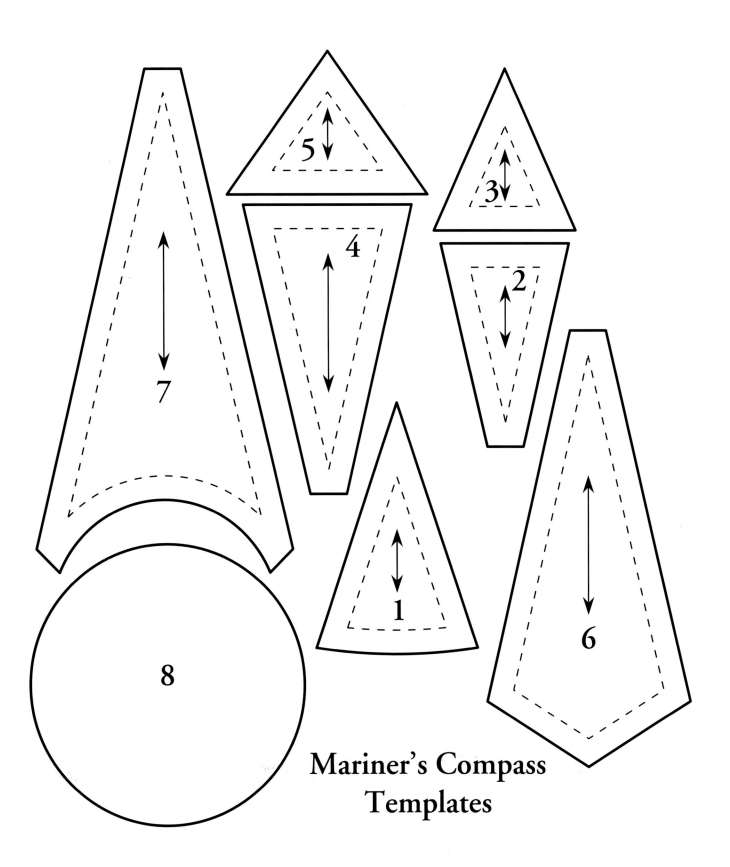

Mariner's Compass
Templates